Special Thanks To Friends Who Supported
And Helped This Book

FIX AMERICA
—IN—
EIGHT YEARS

by

Jeff Lumin

TABLE OF CONTENTS

Chapter 1 - Cut Corporate Income Tax To Bring Back Factories

America is "a shining city on a hill", Reagan addressed millions Americans passionately and optimistically on Nov 3rd, 1980, the eve of election. "Many of us are unhappy about our worsening economic problems, about the constant crisis atmosphere in our foreign policy, about our diminishing prestige around the globe, about the weakness in our economy and national security that jeopardizes world peace, about our lack of strong, straight-forward leadership. And many Americans today, just as they did 200 years ago, feel burdened, stifled and sometimes even oppressed by government that has grown too large, too bureaucratic, too wasteful, too unresponsive, too uncaring about people and their problems."

The victory of Reagan and his revolution seemed ancient to new generations, but his inspiring words, unshakable confidence, and exuberant optimism inspired the nation, and ushered in economic growth and Cold War victory that changed the course of the nation from social turmoil in 60s, and economic drudgery in 70s. After being in White House, Reagan harnessed runaway inflation, strengthened military, and revitalized economic growth. America was on its strong footing again.

Nevertheless, the problems of our economy and society are far severe and devastating than those during Reagan years. Irresponsible politicians have accumulated astronomic debt that will surely hamper future generations; Our once almighty manufacturing prowess has entirely lost to rivaling countries; Our trade deficits are astronomic as nearly everything is made in overseas; Jobs in all industries have moved offshore, leaving millions on welfares and food stamps. Americans are angry and upset than they have ever been!

America needs a revolution, a revolution to restore our values, rebuild labor force, and renew industrial production. In the 2005 CIA report, "Mapping the Global Future: Report of the National Intelligence Council's 2020 Project", CIA concluded that: "The United States will see its relative power position eroded". That alarm had little impact on Congress and our government, and nothing has been done. America has been the land of dream, freedom, and prosperity. But partisan impasses and sold-out politicians had wasted trillions on wrong programs, and angered those productive and innovative Real Americans, who hold our Christian values, pay taxes, and defend the nation!

We need "bold colors", not "pale pastels", as Reagan said when he was the Governor of California. Without immediate and drastic measures, the society is disintegrating into unrest and chaos. National interests have been betrayed and lost by interest groups, bureaucrats and politicians. Beneficiaries of the current system, Washington establishments and Wall Street bankers, are deeply resistant to changes. This new revolution will not win easily, and has to be fought hard. Otherwise, that shining city someday may dim its lights and collapse on the hills.

America is the "last best hope of man on earth!" as Reagan told us. Betrayed politicians and foreign rivals are undermining the hill America was built on - like billions of ants eat a tree. The foundations of this great nation are under severe attacks to dim the shining lights, to weakened our economy and our military. If Americans do not take immediate actions, we will lose the last hope!

Stop Moving Offshore, Start Hiring in USA!

Outsourcing American jobs has been ongoing for decades, exacerbated by the financial crisis. In recent years, outsourcing reached an unprecedented level that jobs of all kinds in the US economy vanished to overseas. It is no surprise that unemployment rate remained high despite fiscal stimulus. And trade deficit kept skyrocketing. America has lost 8.6 million jobs since the 2008 financial crisis. Unemployment rate hit 10% in 2009 as reported, while actual unemployment was at least 16%, because millions quit job searches, took part-time positions or early retirement.

When low-pay manufacturing jobs were offshored in 80s, CNN's economists told us that those jobs were low-pay and low-tech jobs that Americans did not want. Nowadays, jobs are lost in services and in high-techs alike. America is losing millions jobs in high tech with high pays, such as making cell phone, TV and computer, making pharmaceuticals and medical devices, and serving banking customers and IT support. While manufacturing jobs disappeared from US into Asian countries, it did not seem alarming and damaging at the beginning. However, "Between 2001 and 2010, US companies were forced to shutter more than 42,000 factories. A third of all manufacturing jobs, - a full 5.5 million – have disappeared" (*Make It In America*, 2011, Andrew Liveris). 42,000 factories!

When massive containers ships arrive in Los Angeles ports, American jobs were shipped back to Asia, factories in America are closed, and trade deficits are accumulated. People who used to make clothes, shoes, computers, and cars are now on the street! When Clinton signed upon NAFTA and WTO in 90s, did he promise job creations for Americans? It is time to reverse the course of globalization, and rebuild the nation's long-term prosperity. Damages to US economy by this globalization cult are devastating, as ever-more American companies build their factories on foreign soils and hire foreign workers.

Despite $787 billion fiscal rescue package, job market barely recovered. Those losses are permanent, because workers were not cyclically discharged, but secularly offshored to foreign countries.

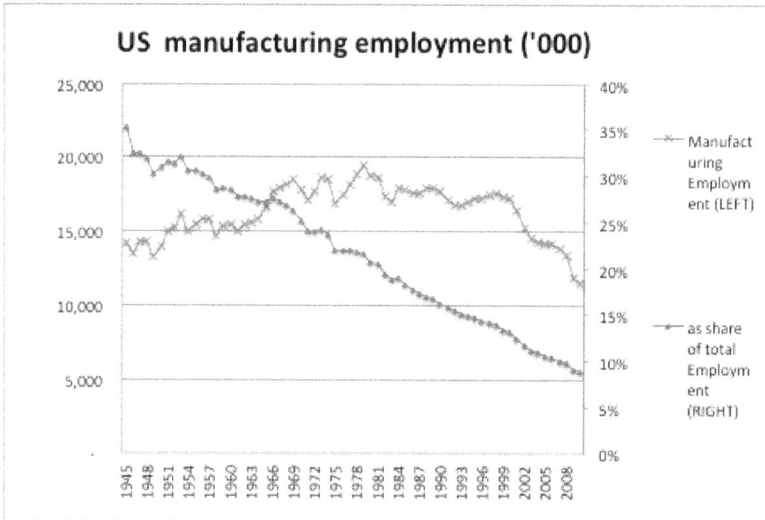

US manufacturing employment ('000)

Source: Department of Labor, BLS

Globalization destroyed the once prosperous middle-class in America. According to data from the Federal Reserve Bank, the percentage of income earned by top 0.1% population rose from 2% in 1980s to near 7% in 2004. A World Bank report in 2001 found that, in 7 out of 8 metrics, "incomes in the lower decile of world income distribution have probably fallen absolutely since the 1980s."

UN published Gini Index, which measures the income distribution, also showed worsening income inequality. "Since

1980 the gap between the earnings of the top fifth and the bottom fifth has jumped by almost 50 percent. The United States is by some measures the most unequal society in the rich world and the most unequal that it's been since the 1920s." Manufacturing boom post World War II created a large middle class, which became the mainstream of American society. Now, they are disappeared into "have" and "have not" categories.

"Middle-income neighborhoods -- where families earn 80 to 120 percent of the local median income -- have plunged by more than 20 percent as a share of all neighborhoods in Baltimore, Chicago, Los Angeles and Philadelphia. They are down 10 percent in the Washington area." (*Blaine Harden,* June 22, 2006)

The rich became richer, and the poor became poorer. Shareholders and senior management of the corporate America benefited from offshoring. Operating margins of S&P 500 companies improved consistently, rising from 4% in 90s to 10% in recent years. There is no doubt that productivity gain in US also helped improving margins, but offshoring and labor cost cut, contributed significantly to the margin.

Why Companies Moved Offshore?

Corporations are economic animals, which take measures to maximize economic interests. Usually, business managers build financial models to compare options when they need to build a plant or enter a new market. They have to consider labor, tax, tariff, healthcare, regulation, supply chain etc. Very often, tax is the heavyweight swing factor when companies choose the offshore or onshore option.

Labor cost differential between USA and overseas is obvious, but nothing much can be done. Even after decades of economic growth and rising wages, Chinese labors, with equal or better skills, are still at a fraction cost of American workers. On average, labor costs in US companies often account for about 1/3 to 1/2 of its total costs. Hence, companies have incentives to move operations offshore to arbitrage the labor cost differential.

Complex and unfair tax and regulatory burdens have "driven the reinsurance business out of the country"; "blocked new gasoline refineries from being built in the US for three decades"; and "driven chemical industry jobs overseas" (*Real Change*, Newt Gingrich). Those complex regulations - environment, labor condition, minimal wage - add compliance costs and drive away businesses from US soil.

Finally, corporate tax is the key driver for corporations to move offshore. For example, corporate tax rate in Ireland is 12.5%, and in US it is 35%. By moving operations (or simple changes of company's domicile location, with no physical change of operation) to offshore, corporate can keep extra 22.5% profits. Of course, the boardroom of corporate made the decision quickly – go offshore!

Additionally, many countries provide incentives and subsidies to attract new business, such as low cost loan, tax holiday, free land, etc. In a world of global competition, countries behave like corporations. Growing economy and creating jobs make politicians popular and powerful. Politicians jet around the world to allure corporations to invest factory in their territories, on many occasions, state head personally deliver the sales pitch to Wall Street.

On sharp contrast, American politicians are doing the opposite to businesses: more regulation and compliance, more taxes and healthcare cost.

When Angela Merkel and Nicolas Sarkozy met with CEOs, they ask how to attract investments to their countries. When Obama met with CEOs, he asked for donations to his next election.

A deep ditch between US government and business, deeply entrenched in the ideology to separate business from government, has created a prosperous free market economy with minimal government intervention, the *laissez-faire* principle, has worked.

However, the global business environment changed. Other countries are much more eager and friendly in attracting new investment. Nowadays, CEOs are sought after by politicians with tax break, low rate loan, free land, on a global scale. Of those incentives, corporate tax rate is the particularly powerful tool. Lowering corporate tax rate to 12.5% has made Ireland an instant attractive destination for manufacturing. Almost every large multi-national corporation, from Merck, Pfizer, Dell, Microsoft, to Siemens, ABB, GlaxoSmithKline, have manufacturing in Ireland. (or at least tax identity in Ireland)

Top Corporate Income Tax Rates in the OECD, 2010

United States	40.0%
Japan	35.7%
Belgium	34.0%
France	33.3%
Italy	31.4%
Canada	31.0%
Spain	30.0%
New Zealand	30.0%
Mexico	30.0%
Australia	30.0%
Germany	29.4%
Luxembourg	28.6%
Norway	28.0%
Britain	28.0%
Sweden	26.3%
Finland	26.0%
Netherlands	25.5%
Portugal	25.0%
Israel	25.0%
Denmark	25.0%
Austria	25.0%
Korea	24.2%
Greece	24.0%
Switzerland	21.2%
Estonia	21.0%
Turkey	20.0%
Slovenia	20.0%
Slovakia	19.0%
Poland	19.0%
Hungary	19.0%
Czech Rep.	19.0%
Iceland	18.0%
Chile	17.0%
Ireland	12.5%

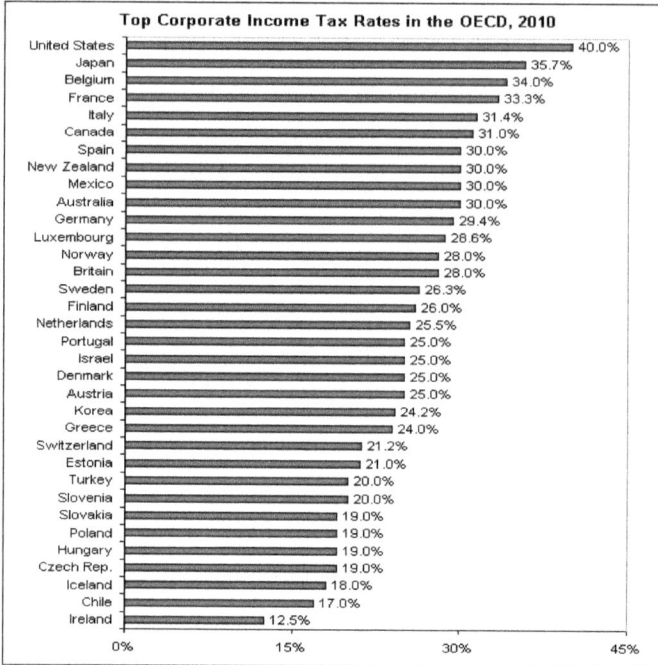

Source: CATO Institute

Cutting Corporate Tax Is Not "Trickle Down" Economy

If we reduce the corporate tax rate, we can make a big difference on economic growth today. While labor cost is the obvious excuse for offshoring, very often it is the tax that drives company offshore. Nevertheless, it is difficult to sell the idea of cutting corporate tax, when national debt and deficit are at record levels. Corporate America is viewed as grossly rich and greedy. Why should we cut tax bill for corporates? Make the rich richer?

No, the truth is paradoxical. Cutting corporate income tax actually encourages new business startup, new jobs creation, and eventually increases tax revenues. When companies conduct analysis to choose location for a new plant or a startup, they calculate and compare NPV (net present value), and ROIC (return on invested capital) financial indicators. The low tax rate in offshore countries significantly enhances the project's NPV value. By keeping corporate tax high, America has pushed established corporates and new ventures alike to offshore.

Cutting corporate tax is not "trickle down" gimmicks to enrich the fat corporations, as many Leftist claimed. Jobs are mostly created or cut by SMEs, not so by big corporations like IBM, Citi and Exxon. Those mom-pop shops are most sensitive to economic condition and tax rate. Many times, tax can eat most of their profits. Cutting tax will boost their profits and hiring significantly. By maintaining US tax rate at 35% (39% if include state tax), politicians are telling corporates "Go ahead moving to China. We do not care about your business".

A 2008 KPMG report demonstrated that US corporate tax is 14% points higher than the global average, and nearly 17% points higher than the average among European Union nations. High tax

drove away business. How long can we wait when jobs are
bleeding out of America?

In the meantime, corporate tax revenue is 2010 was $190 billion,
9% of total US tax revenue. Although not insignificant portion, it
is not very meaningful to the overall deficit, if reduce tax rate to
10%. Plus, government spending in 2010 was 146% of tax
revenue. Cutting corporate tax would have little affect on deficit,
since Obama spend like a drunken sailor anyway.

If tax rate is reduced to 10% range, loss of revenue will be
negligible and will be temporary, because new jobs will return to
US. Newly employed people will pay tax, will spend and
consume, will buy houses and cars. Entire value creations at the
local economy will far exceed initial loss of corporate tax revenue.

While the combined US federal and state tax rate for corporate is
39%, the average of effective tax rate for 1,000 large corporations
is about 27%. How could that happen?

First, there are many loopholes and tax breaks for corporations,
which were heavily lobbied by special interest groups with
myriads of excuses. Because the benefit to that special industry
or company was so tremendous, and the loss of revenue is small
relatively to overall pie of corporate tax, companies are
incentivized to spend on making tax exceptions. For example,
airline industry may lobby for $300 million special tax credit in
one year, which is equivalent $1 per capita in US, Congress may
be convinced that tax credit is necessary to keep the airline strong
and competitive because we all have to travel, right?

Because potential benefits of lobbying are simply tremendous,
many interest groups spend heavily to lobby for special tax
treatment. This created market places for open corruption.

Public are not aware of and not agitated by those special tax codes, since each share only slightly increased tax burden. Overtime, special tax treatments aggregated into world's most complex and unfair tax codes.

Second, an overseas division of US corporations pays the local tax. If the local tax rate is lower than domestic rate, companies do not have to pay the statutory US tax rate IF the company keeps the profits in overseas division. The company has to pay the Treasure the differences in tax when the cash is repatriated to US headquarter. Those accumulated foreign earnings have exceeded $1 trillions dollars as of 2011!

What this rule does is to motivate US companies to keep their overseas profits in overseas divisions – reinvest and grow, and create jobs and prosperity on foreign land!

Are our tax codes written by a patriotic Congress or by traitors working for foreign interests?

What Should Be Changed? Cut Corporate Tax!

On so called "untaxed foreign earnings" in overseas divisions, we can either tax those profits at US statutory rate regardless of location, or we can make the tax holiday permanent for companies to repatriate the cash, or reduce domestic tax rate equivalent to most foreign countries!

The first measure will create a rainfall of tax revenue, but will drive companies to be domiciled in overseas (tax inversion); and the second one will motivate companies to bring the cash back to US on a window of opportunity. The worst is doing nothing: the current rule has prevented the huge pool of cash to be reinvested in US to help our still-struggling economy. Accounting to The Analyst's Accounting Observer, the untaxed foreign earnings are over $1trillions by large US corporations as of 2011.

If we had brought those money back, US would not waste the unprecedented $787 billion fiscal stimulus plan by Obama! Private spending and investing are more efficient and productive than government spending.

Even more ridiculous and unfair about the US tax codes is that they treat corporates favorably and individuals unfavorably. Personal tax codes require all US citizens to pay US statutory tax rate no matter where on earth he/she worked during the year. If the US citizen working on foreign countries, and local tax rate is lower than US rate, the person is liable to pay the difference to IRS (no matter whether the person repatriates the cash or not). In a similar situation for a corporation, the corporation does not have to pay the US tax rate. Corporates have much more clout in lobbying IRS than individuals working overseas, because expatriate are a small minority of the society?!

By reducing statutory tax rate, companies' investment decisions will be recalibrated. New companies, and millions SMEs, will be attracted to be domicile domestically. Cutting corporate tax will create jobs instantly.

This strategy is very similar to Reagan's two tax cuts in and 1981 and 1986.The Economic Recovery Tax Act of 1981 cut individual tax rates by 23%, which was phased-in over 3 years. The individual top marginal rates were cut from 70% to 50% and the bottom rate dropped from 14% to 11%.

The Tax Reform Act of 1986 reduced corporate tax rate from 50% to 40%, meaningfully lower than OECD countries' (see chart below). Individual marginal tax was further reduced from 50% to 28%. 1986 tax reform simplified tax codes, reduced tax shelters and tax brackets

On Oct 22, 1986, Reagan made a speech on the South Lawn of the White House:
"In a moment I will be sitting at that desk, taking up a pen and signing the most sweeping overhaul of our tax code in our nation's history. When I sign this bill into law,
America will have the lowest marginal tax rates and the most modern tax code among major industrialized nations, one that encourages risk-taking, innovation, and that old American spirit of enterprise. We'll be refueling the American growth economy with the kind of incentives that helped create record new business and nearly 11.7 million jobs in just 46 months."

Source: White House. President Reagan signed the "Tax Reform Act of 1986" on the South Lawn.

While some might criticize that Reagan tax cuts worsened US budget deficits, Reagan supporters believed tax cuts triggered the 1980s economic expansion that eventually lowered the annual deficits.

However, the tax advantages for America companies disappeared, when other countries lowered tax. From 1996 to 2010, major European economies have reduced corporate tax rate from 38% to 24% (Source: CATO Institute). After a recent cut of corporate tax in Japan, US become the world champion in corporate tax rate. It is very ironic that America is supposed to the most capitalistic and business-friendly in the world.

Statutory U.S. Corporate Tax Rate
Compared to OECD Averages
1981 to 2012

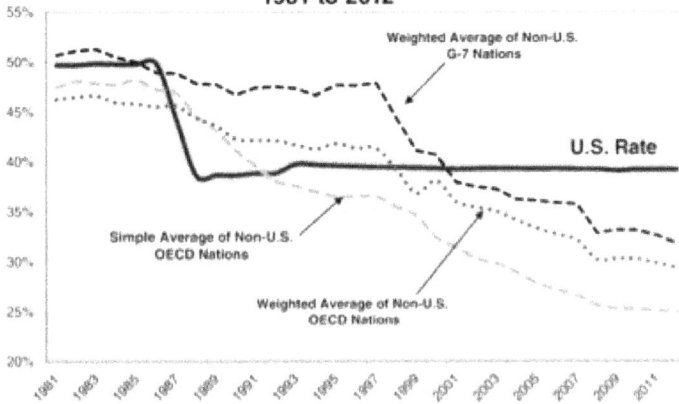

Source: Tax Foundation calculations based on OECD and IMF data

Britain or Germany - Which Country Shall America Follow?

High labor cost should NOT be the excuse for America to lose manufacturing jobs to China, because labor costs in both Germany and Japan are more expensive than that in US. However, Germany and Japan have maintained their share in global manufacturing. While low-end manufacturing moved to China and Eastern Europe, Germany and Japan have retained their competitiveness in high-end manufacturing, which in turn kept their foreign trade in surplus, and preserved a strong and healthy mid-class in their economies.

UK built the world strongest manufacturing sector in 19th century following the Industrial Revolution. In 1860, at the Zenith of Victoria Reign, UK produced 53% of world steel, 50% of coal, and consumed just under half of world cotton. (Source: *The Rise and Fall of the Great Powers,* Paul Kennedy, P151). With about 2% of the world population, UK's manufacturing capacity accounted for 40-45% of the world capacity. During the era, UK was the unchallenged world industrial and commercial superpower.

The tide turned after the World War I. UK abandoned manufacturing and its economy shifted to service and banking. From 1955 to 1976, UK's share of world trade fell from 19.8% to 8.7%. Its share of world manufactured products fell from 8.6% to 4.0 from 1953 to 1980. With declining of manufacturing capacity and of the number of working class, UK economy has been hit hard repeatedly in post-WWII recessions. By 1980, manufacturing has fallen to 31% of GDP, and was worsened further to 13% in 2008.

The lesson of "the English disease" should be awakening to Americans. Shockingly, the America has not wakened up to the alarm. If we continue on this path, the shining city on the hill will lose its lights. For decades, we took for granted the drain of manufacturing jobs, while "elite economists" lied to us it did not matter - people would find jobs in other sectors. What sectors are there new jobs?

The opposite has been true in Germany where manufacturing has the stronghold. Built on ruins after World War II, the country has build the world's best manufacturing capabilities. The country's trade balance has been reversed from $6 billion deficit in 1998 to $267 surplus in 2008. With 1.2% of global population, Germany generates 17% of world industrial output. (Source: *Make It In America*, p27) Germany's strong, high quality manufacturing sector has kept the economy strong and unemployment low during the financial crisis.

The lesson we can learn from UK and Germany should be obvious. The importance of manufacturing is multi-faceted. Not only it is necessary for building a healthy economy, creating jobs and wealth, and prevention of income inequality, but also for national security, strong currency and good trade relationship. In 1950s, manufacturing accounted for 28% of GDP in US, and today that number is 12%. It is shocking that, as the world's most developed and wealthiest country (not in term of Treasury's bank account), America did not produce: 1 cell phone (1.8 billion units sold worldwide in 2009) and 1 LCD TV panel (220 million units sold in 2009). Our country cannot give up manufacturing, otherwise we will lose out entirely.

Additionally, manufacturing creates jobs through its value chain, ranging from mining, energy, transportation, to communication, packing, and retailing. In the chart by the Manufacturing Institute, $1 dollar sales of manufactured product generate $1.4 of output in other sectors. This multiplying effect of manufacturing is much stronger than other industries, particularly services.

How could our country afford the life style and consumption when America is producing less and less industrial products? Printing IOU - Treasury bills is disastrous economic model. It will bring America to the ruin! Who will lend us money to buy cars, TVs, iPhones, houses, when we produce almost nothing to trade with them? We already owe $14.3 trillion debt!

Lucky enough that we can still make F-35 and aircraft carriers, but we already lost our production capacity in building large-scale steel structures for nuclear reactors, for long range bridges, and for ocean-drilling platforms, and for many others. The pride and grand victory of American military during the World War II was built upon industrial power. Following the decline of our industrial power, can our military power be sustained?

America Can Improve Productivity and Compete on Manufacturing Again!

Longer term, productivity gain hold the key to revitalize American manufacturing, and job market in general. Fortunately, the cost gap between US and China's workforce has been shrinking. Productivity gain will offset the disadvantage of American workers. A report by the Boston Consulting Group (BCG) forecasts that, "by 2015 – on the back of good productivity growth and relatively low wages – the US is likely to be slightly ahead of China as a base for making many of the goods destined for sale in North America." (Source: Financial Times, May 5th, 2011, Peter Marsh)

A Chinese industrial worker produces $12,642 worth of output in 2005 (almost eight times more than in 1980), and a US manufacturing employee produced an unprecedented $104,606 of value in 2005. Using steel industry as an example, on average one steel worker of America produces 1,023 tons of steel, and one Chinese steel worker, 253 tons! Over the past 30 years, American steel producers have, in some cases, reduced the number of work-hours required to produce a ton of steel by 90%.

Equally impressive is the energy efficiency of American steel industry, to produce 1 ton of steel, American mills use 170 kg of coking coal, and Chinese mills, 710 kg. Indeed, The US steel industry has the lowest energy consumption and lowest CO_2 emissions per ton of any steel producing industry in the world. The US steel industry has reduced its energy intensity by 30% since 1990.

"Hal Sirkin of Boston Consulting Group says rising wages in China are dulling its edge as a low-wage nirvana. In 2000, wages of Chinese production workers averaged 3% of what their

American counterparts made. Today, they are at 9%. BCG expects the figure to reach 17% by 2015. Mr. Sirkin predicts that will prompt some manufacturers to move jobs back to the U.S." (Wall Street Journal, July 27, 2011)

American labor force is highly productive, innovative and competitive. With tax cut and deregulation, America can regain its manufacturing power. America cannot lose on manufacturing. And it is not too late yet!

Chapter 2 - Raise Border Tax To Balance Trade With Every Nation

"Proposals to return jobs to the US are economically non-viable," Contractor concludes. "Disruption of global value chains would add hundreds of billions per year to US businesses, increasing prices for US buyers – with extra costs falling disproportionately on lower-income Americans." (Farok Contractor, Rutgers University)

Apparently, Professors Contractor believed that low-income Americans prefer to be jobless and able to buy Nike shoes at $40 made in overseas, rather than have a job, have a salary, and buy the Nike shoes at $80 dollar. This economist is a genius! It is true that some consumer goods price will rise if productions are shifted to US soils, but keeping supply chain offshore have dumped millions Americans from factory floors to the street.

While Americans suffer from job loss and poverty, declining real income and degradation of living standard, those "spokesman" economists, hired by interest group, continued lying how Americans benefit from global trade on CNN and university classroom.

"Most advanced economies have become primarily service economies. Rich countries are service economies, focused on finance, engineering, design and health care, and this is dictated by their comparative advantage." Gaur and Mudambi urge politicians to reject the fallacies and citizens to make informed decisions before voting" (Gaur and Mudambi, YaleGlobal)

What a lie! Because America is an "advanced" economy, hence, we have the "comparative advantage" of high unemployment, huge debt, poverty at bottom, and trade deficit that "selling the nation out from under us" (Warren Buffet 2003)?!

The biggest enemy often is not the foreign adversary, but the enemy inside - the Democrats, the Congressmen/women, big corporation's lobbyists, and spokesman economists - who work for foreign interests to undermine America's economic strengths. They are around us - on CNN, on NY Times, in our Congress, and in corporate suites.

Trade Deficit Ruined Job Market And US Economy

Trade deficit in 2010 hit a record of $646 billions; and trade deficits accumulated from 2001 to 2010 were over $6.5 trillion! During the period, while America accumulated $6.5 trillion of trade deficits, China has amassed $3 trillion dollar reserves, Japan $1.1 trillion, and Germany $160 billion. It is the biggest wealth transfer in human history. Those dollar reserves by foreign countries are near mortgage on entire American homes.

Since the start of 2008 financial crisis, 8.6 million of jobs have been lost and unemployment rate hit 10%, with more than half of the job loss were from manufacturing. If we continue on this path, America is heading to be destitute. We have lost entirely the economic warfare, but our elected politicians have turned deaf ear to all those alarms.

Immediately, we should implement tariff on goods from all countries, starting at 30% and adjust until trade balance is fully restored. Or we can implement a scaled tariff at 0%-40%, and rank all country by trade deficit as percentage of total trade (trade deficit/(export+import). Higher the percentage scale, higher the tariff. If balance is not reached with that country, raise the tariff until trade balance is reached. We should balance trade with each and every country on earth!

Even if we tariff all imports at 10%, the tariff revenue in 2010 would have been $240 billion, more than enough to eliminate the entire corporate income tax - $184 billion! If corporate tax were eliminated, investments of new factories on US soil would soar and create jobs in millions.

If we make equivalent goods on US soil that is worth the $646 billion deficit, and assume each workers produces $100,000 value per year, **6 millions jobs** would be created overnight! In 2011, total manufacturing employment was only 12 million in US. (At GE, $470,000 revenue per employee. $220,000 at Walmart, and $240,000 at IBM.) This move would bring unemployment to zero! Actually, labor shortage in USA!

Despite all those "if", none has been done to restore manufacturing and reduce deficit by Obama, except his popular slogans and eloquent, empty speeches. Real income growth for all American workers has stalled. "From 1988 to 2011, average annual growth for this group was 0.5 percent in the United States and Germany, 1.7 percent in France and 1.9 percent in the United Kingdom. Over the same period, the middle deciles in urban and rural China have grown by 6 and 8 percent per annum, respectively, 4 percent in Thailand and 8 percent in Vietnam. Broadly, the average income growth of a median household in Asia was about four times as high as one in the West" (Branko Milanovic)

The job loss in many states is so dire that it is hard to believe: New York and Ohio lost 38% of manufacturing job from 2000 to 2010, while New Jersey lost 39%, Michigan 48% during the same period.

US Trade Balance 1978-2010
($ million)

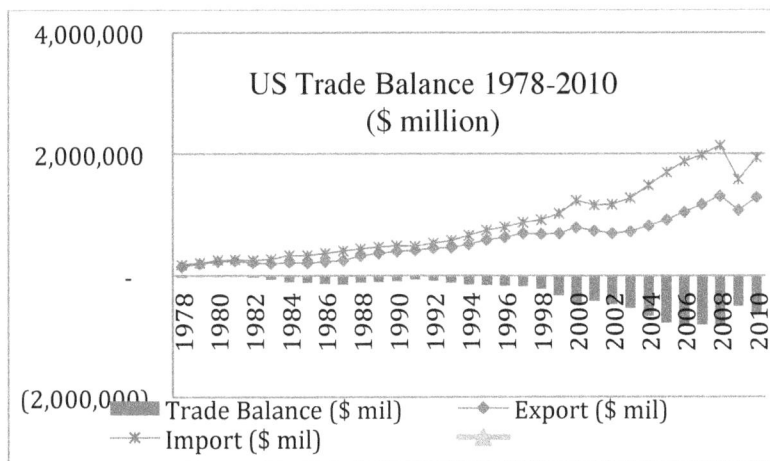

Source: Dept. of Commerce, Fed Reserve Bank of St. Louis.

1973 was the last year when US import exceeded export. Since then, US trade has been on an ever-rising, spiral deficit each and every year. The old glories of Ford Mustang, Kodak film, Polaroid camera, Apple Mac II... are long gone, when "Made in America" means innovation, novelty, quality, and fashion that envied by the world.

Trade deficit and job loss were caused by massive closeout of manufacturing plants through the US. Although liberal economist, such as Robert Reich, continued denied that job loss was caused by outsourcing, because "Productivity keeps growing, as do corporate profits. But jobs and wages are not growing."

According to a study by Economic Policy Institute, from 1998 to 2007, more than 3.2 million manufacturing jobs were lost by unfavorable trade relationship. When America border are open and free to foreign imports, domestic workers are heading to welfares and food stamps. A quick look at shelves at Wal-Mart Stores will explains all those, no need for Ivy leagues economics professors. Highly correlated move of US current account balance and manufacturing trade balance, demonstrated by Robert E. Scott of Economic Policy Institute, unequivocally proved that US trade deficits were caused by loss of manufacturing.

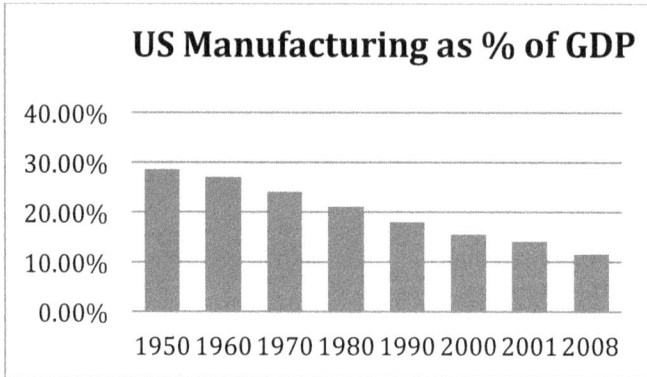

US Manufacturing as % of GDP

40.00%	
30.00%	
20.00%	
10.00%	
0.00%	

1950 1960 1970 1980 1990 2000 2001 2008

Source: U.S. Department of Commerce, Bureau of Economic Analysis

Transitioning to service economy was hailed as "new paradigm" and "comparative advantage", without any sympathy for Americans losing industrial jobs. While the productivity gain in American manufacturing is truly remarkable: post World War II - manufacturing output increased 6.8 times from 1950 to 2008, while employment in manufacturing stayed constant, in a range of 14-19 million people. (until recent years, employment number dropped to 11 million)

Manufacturing has been on a downhill for decades - manufacturing as percentage of GDP has dropped from 29% in 1950 to 12% in 2008; People employed on factory floors have declined from 35% in 1950 to 9% in 2008 as share of total employment.

How did we get into this trade deficit mess? Can we rebalance our trade?

Globalization Caused Economic Suicide of America

Globalization became the economic religion after fall of Berlin
Wall in 1989, when the ideology fight was over and new mission
was to build a one-world market. During the Cold War, trades
were limited to each side of the superpower, with the purpose of
strengthening connections inside the bloc, and of fighting the
other side of power. During 80s, western corporations were
saddled with weak demand, high inflation and high labor cost.
Fall of Soviet Union and opening of global markets breezed
much-needed hopes to Multi National corporations (MNC).
MNC have incentives to open borders, lower tariffs, cut
regulations, hire cheap labors, so that trades can be truly "free"
and profits can soar.

At the end of World War II, while IMF and World Bank were
established to implement monetary policies, a third planned UN
agency, International Trade Organization, to regulate and manage
global trade, did not come to its birth. Instead, 23 countries
signed GATT as a provisional, multilateral agreement to reduce
tariff in 1947. During 1947 and 1994, eight rounds of trade
negotiation occurred among members. The Uruguay Round,
lasted from 1986 to 1994, culminated in comprehensive trade
agreement and establishment of a formal organization, WTO, in
Jan 1995. The agreement covered areas far beyond the GATT
scope, including goods, service, intellectual property, investment.

With all essential ingredients in place, global trades boomed.
World exports as of total gross world product rose from 8.5% in
1970, to 17.2% in 2009. The world was open for business, and
sky was the only limit.

Those MNC needed a spokesperson to voice their plan. The most
prominent scholar to lecture Americans, who were "startlingly

crude and ill-informed", and to alleviate their "ignorant" fear of job loss, was Paul Krugman, who won Nobel price for his work on trade theory. No one had more credentials to teach Americans about global trade.

In August 1994 issue of Harvard Business Review, he wrote "The truth, however, is that fears about the economic impact of Third World competition are almost entirely unjustified." And he continued, "America's growing links with the rest of the world are not responsible for slower average income growth, higher unemployment, or the productivity slowdown. The charge that American workers and companies must compete on an unlevel international playing field reflects a misunderstanding of what trade and exchange are all about."

However, by early 2000s, the facts and evidences were so strong that the fear of job less by union and manufacturing workers turned into the worst nightmares: jobs were gone, income were down, and factories were ruined across America. As Kevin Danaher wrote in his book, "The increasing globalization of U.S. corporations gives them the leverage to hold down wages and resist unionization. Average real wages (corrected for inflation) have been falling since the early 1970s. By 1992, average weekly earnings in the private, non-agricultural part of the U.S. economy were 19 percent below their peak in the early 1970s. Nearly one-fourth of the U.S. workforce now earns less in real terms than the 1968 minimum wage!" (*Globalization and the Downsizing of the American Dream*)

How could Krugman was so wrong for so long? And even worse, nothing has been done by our elected politicians to stop our economic suicide?

Comparative advantage theory by David Ricardo has been well studied by generations of economists. American economy, being the world's most advanced, should open its market to all countries, if they meet certain criteria, as preached by liberal economists. Free trade would improve market efficiency globally and creates wealth and prosperity, and "Open trade is not just an economic opportunity, it is a moral imperative. Trade creates jobs for the unemployed. When we negotiate for open markets, we're providing new hope for the world's poor. And when we promote open trade, we are promoting political freedom." President Bush said in a 2001 speech.

What they missed was that third world workers were well trained and highly skilled, at a small fraction of cost. Not only they grabbed low-end manufacturing quickly, but also climbed on the value chain of technological advancement and knowledge-based skills. The blind believing in American superiority in technology and innovation turned to be misleading and wrong. Global trade in a free market mechanism was believed to shed the low-end of US economy to the third world when the America migrated to the high end and service economy. The migration and outsourcing were supposed to improve the efficiency of all participants, but proved to be detrimental to American workers and worsened income gap.

"While globalization has led to benefits for some, it has not led to benefits for all. The benefits appear to have gone to those who already have the most, while many of the poorest have failed to benefit fully and some have even been made poorer." (*A Human Development Approach to Globalisation*, Duncan and Melamed)

It is almost right. Indeed, the biggest losers in this round globalization were the middle class Americans, who have prospered from and since Henry Ford invented assembly lines, and build American industrial prowess by their hands. When their factories packed and left for overseas, they were swept to unemployment queues and food stamps.

Keynesian demand management becomes even more critical in today's global economy, which is characterized by overcapacity of labor and capital. No longer valid is the scarcity principle, upon which classic economics theories are built on. Labor supply is almost unlimited after integrating China and India into the world markets. Capital can be printed at will by the Federal Reserve Bank and by other central banks. The limit on the world economy is the end-demand.

The most valuable resources of global economies are American consumers, who are willing to spend and willing to borrow. In a world with overcapacity plus high saving, demand limits growth. Demand is hard to find, but supply is abundant.

Ray Kurzweil, in his book *"The Singularity is Near"*, expected that the speed of technology adoption would continue accelerating; changes we will experience in the decade will be equivalent to 200 years of changes at current speed. Productivity gain will worsen the issue of global overcapacity. He illustrated that it took 45 years for telephone to reach 50% of household, 40 year for radio; color TV went to 50% of household living in 10 years.

Today, smart phone reached 50% of population in 10 years, and for Facebook, 5 years.

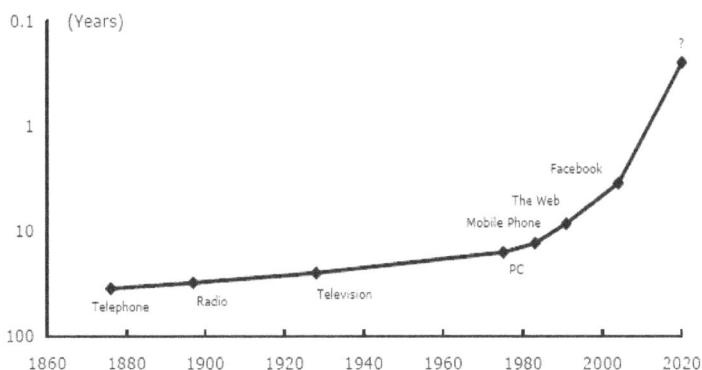

Source: Ray Kurzweil, *The Singularity is near*

Scarcity to economy is like hunger to human body. Biologically, human body is engineered to efficiently absorb and utilize scarce nutrition. When food becomes abundant - high fat, high sugar, and high protein "delicacy" becomes new normal, we are swallowing obesity, heart disease, diabetes, and liver problem. When rate is low, capital floods and asset bubbles. Cheap labor and cheap capital combined to form excessive capacities; global markets become bloated and wasteful. In last hundreds of years, population growth eventually engrossed any excessive capacities. This time, it may not happen again, as the world population plateaus.

Under Clinton's open border and free trade mantra, US was flooded with goods made from all over the world, particularly from developing countries. American consumers brought hope, boom and wealth to people in the third world, but leave jobless and hopeless at home.

Globalization has not been a win-win situation for all. "The US effectively accepted the role of "buyer of last resort" for the world's over-capacity, every year buying and borrowing more from abroad than it produced at home. That is where the trade deficits and swelling debt came from and the rising inequality. They all persist under Obama." (William Greider, *The Nation Correspondent*)

While America is often criticized for its dollar hegemony and for printing greenbacks to buy foreign goods, those critics forget that it is America greenbacks bringing prosperity to their economies. What William Kristol called American "benevolent global hegemony" has brought unprecedented economic boom in developing countries. The most successful newly industrialized economies, Japan and South Korea, and recently China, were all kick-started by exporting to America. With the dollar they earned, they bought new machinery, hired workers, and upgraded factories, expanded to new markets and so on.

Unfair Trade Agreement and Japanese Auto market

Does America benefit from globalization in the last decade? No, absolutely not. To millions American, free trade means job loss. Those preach by liberal economists that globalization benefit Americans as they can buy cheap shoes and TV at Walmart, are absolutely lies!

Globalization has done much more harm than good to America. To the disappointment of Joseph Stiglitz, chairman of Bill Clinton's Council of Economic Advisers and then chief economist at the World Bank, he was so concerned those trade agreements in 90s were designed and enforced by America to serve its interests. "The job of Western trade negotiators is to get a better trade deal for their countries' industries," as he claimed in his book *"Make Globalization Work"*. Those rules would favor America and further impoverish people in the Third World. Poor countries have gotten back too little from trade deals, he said. They should be given free access to rich-country markets, and the fat countries should quit featherbedding their farmers.

Opposite happened. Americans lost job, and lost income, and our nations is deeply in debt!

Free trade and a win-win fantasy are based on numerous idealistic fantasies of liberal economists - fair and sufficient competitions, no export subsidies, no currency manipulation, no violation of labor condition, no counterfeit, no piracy of intellectual property, no malicious barrier of entry and so on.

In practice, our trading partners violated nearly ALL those assumptions. They kept their market closed to US products, while stole US market, in all major industries. "Current World Trade Organization rules have been effective at lowering tariffs, but less effective at ensuring an equal regulatory playing field, especially in countries such as China where the government owns many businesses." (*Chris Miller, Yale University*)

Our elected politicians were busy accepting "consulting" fees from those foreign corporations, and our President never honored campaign promises to punish trading partners.

The worst nightmare of trade agreement and market loss is in the US auto market. Despite many rounds of negotiation since Carter Administrations, Japanese auto market is virtually closed to Big Three, by many non-tariff barriers, such as limits on dealership, excessive certification requirement, collaboration with Japan government agency in creating delay and wait in import process, negative PR advertising, strict investment law prohibiting local production.

Nevertheless, despite of efforts by US industry and politicians, US automakers sold only meniscus number of cars in Japan. Chevrolet exported exactly one vehicle to Japan for every 400 Toyotas exported to the US in 2008. If productions at its US plants are counted in, and the ratio became: one Chevrolet vehicle sold in Japan, for every 1,300 Toyota sold in the US.

In Aug 2009, 192 Fords and 63 Chevrolets were sold in Japan. And Toyota sold 1.8 million cars in 2009 at US market. By all measures, the Japanese market is closed to Big Three. In the mean time, domestic market share of Big Three has decreased from 70% to 53% from 1998 to 2008.

Since 2000, US exports to Japan 183,000, versus 16.3 million cars exported from Japan to the America!

The financial crisis punched auto industry with a heavy hit that knocked them out to bankruptcy. Companies' profit margins were already thin or at loss during booming days, and turned red immediately when crisis hit. After approaching the government to seek loans, General Motors published 2008 financial result – a losses of $31 billion after the company lost $39 billion in 2007 when economy was strong. While Ford survived on government loans, Chrysler filed bankruptcy in April 2009 and GM in June 2009.

Not surprisingly, laid-off of workers, closing plants and car models, and reduction of dealership followed bankruptcy filing. Chrysler close 25% of its US dealerships as part of its restructuring process, while GM cut 47,000 jobs in 2009, 19% of its globally workforce. During financial crisis, America autoworkers are laid off; unemployment rose to record; trade deficit with Japan hit a high; and government debt ceiling had to be lifted.

Big Three has long lost their competitiveness since first oil crisis in 1973. Toyota has risen to be the world's largest auto maker with global sales of 9.9 million cars in 2012, and sustained 14% market share in US market, and sold more car in US than in Japan. Corona became all time best selling car with 27 million sold in 140 countries.

Greedy corporate America should take the blame because they moved factories to overseas. But who is responsible for the high tax rate, high healthcare cost, high minimal wage, and no subsidies, no incentives and no barrier for foreign products? Who in Washington is safeguard our national "vital interest"?

It is time to take all actions we can possibly do to attract business back to American soil. Americans need jobs, at all levels. Why should we worry about trade war? We have nothing to lose but reduction of trade deficit!

Should we concern about retaliation? What can they do? Stop selling us clothes and shoes, and no Toyota cars on the road? Time is different from 1929, when US was a trade surplus countries and retaliation by our trade partners negatively affected economic recovery. In 2011, retaliation by our trade partners will reduce trade deficit and create jobs in America.

Our government and business have to work together to find solutions. Our tax code, regulations, healthcare, minimal wage, together disadvantage our corporations and competitiveness. Business are constantly allured to foreign soils. America needs a revolution so that our country and our business can compete in a post-globalization world.

While American is a rule-based society – we do what we say, but foreign countries do NOT follow what they promise on paper. While we open our market to the world, the world does not reciprocate. Our exports were often dis-favored and our products face malicious barriers. Talking about business environment in China, Jeff Immelt, CEO of GE, confessed at a dinner in Rome in July 2010 that: "I am not sure that in the end they want any of us to win, or any of us to be successful." (*Financial Times, July 20, 2010*)

"We are feeling less and less welcome in China, which is why you are seeing more people speaking out and reconsidering their futures in China," said John Neuffer of the US Information Technology Industry Council.

Facing increasing hostile business environments in foreign countries, American corporation failed in overseas markets.

Exports from America stagnated during the two decades of globalization, while imports skyrocketed. American consumers were the growth engines of developing economies, while US job markets shrank and real income flattened.

Nothing can be more shameful and misleading by telling Americans that they benefit from globalization. "The second popular myth is that imports make a country poorer, and a country must export more than it imports to be prosperous. There are two major problems with this view. First, merchandise trade deficits per se, when countries import more goods and services than they export, are not detrimental to economic growth…As long as the domestic economy is an attractive destination for foreign capital, a country can afford to run deficits. Thus, an innovation-driven economy, such as the United States, can support trade deficits year after year, by way of an inflow of foreign capital" (Ajai Gaur and Ram Mudambi, Rutgers University)

This is an example of lunacy taught at our universities, funded by government, and free from guilt by telling lies. With workers on street, and debt piling up, they are saying it is "not detrimental", and "can support trade deficit year after year"?!

How To Balance Trade in 2024

Raise tariff on all imports until full balance of trade is restored! Immediately, we can start with 30% tariff, and adjust the rate annually to reduce deficit to zero. Of the $645 billion trade deficit in 2010, $372 billion were from trading with Asian countries, and $353 billion from importing oil. If we exclude trade of oil and Asian countries, our trade with the rest of world was almost in balance. Hence, we should focus on raising tariff from those deficit-generating countries.

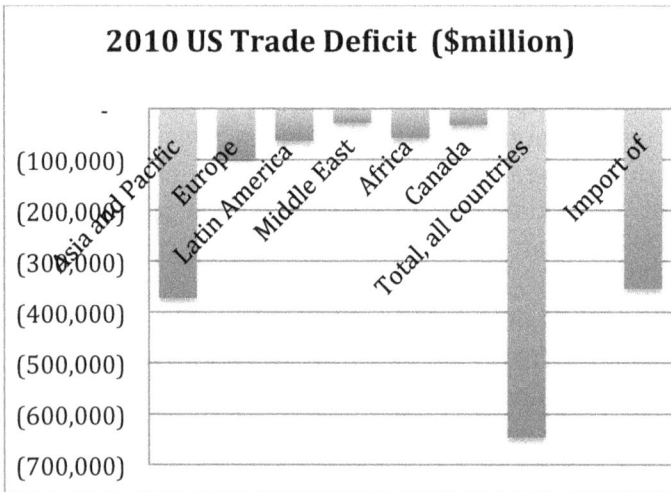

Source: Dept. of Commerce.

To balance our trade, we need a basket of coordinated policies to shape our trade status. Weak dollar is another policy we should adopt to rebuild our manufacturing. President Obama set a goal of doubling our export, and creating 2 million jobs in a 5 year period, at the 2010 State of the Union address. Although that goal is inspiring, it is very lofty and difficult to achieve. Obama is much better at talking than at doing. We will have to wait and see.

First, our dollar is too strong which has to weaken to make our products affordable. Our industrials need to design, develop and produce products more competitively. American pharmaceutical products and (in old days) semiconductor chips are the role model, with strong innovation, strong intellectual property. Tariff and regulation should be in place to facilitate the export and build relationship with trading partners.

While nothing much we can about reliance on imported oil, we can do a lot to improve energy efficiency, developing shale gas and renewables. Many initiatives have been well thought and discussed. To reduce the trade deficit with Asian countries, we need a basket of solutions to bring back manufacturing and investments, not an easy task.

Rebuilding our manufacturing capacity and creating jobs will be critical in reducing our trade balance. We cannot rely on foreigners to make things for us, particularly those critical technologies for defense and communication. America has to be self-sufficient in advanced, precision manufacturing! Given size of population and education level, workers at all levels, from best engineers to factory floor workers, can be easily found in America. It is our anti-business welfare system, tax codes, neglecting of industry development, strong dollar policy, stupidity in trade agreement, and betrayal of Americans' interest that have destroyed our manufacturing.

We even failed to commercialize our best R&D fruits. CEO of Dow Chemical, Andrew Liveris, told an appalling story - "For example, solar panel was developed in 1970s to supply power on satellites. In last thirty years, Dept. of Energy estimated that total R&D spending was over $15 billion to develop solar from a prototype to commercial product. However, the technology was brought to market by Japan, and scaled up incredibly in China.

43

China has built the world largest solar panel industry employed millions people. On the contrary, total employment by solar industry in US is less than 10,000 people. " (Source: Andrew Liveris, *Make It In America*")

Raising tariff and bring back manufacturing will be a tough fight against vested interest groups and big corporations. For example, Hewlett Packard, the iconic technology pioneer in Silicon Valley, and computer power house that supply servers to defense and government, was created by series of mergers of leading computer brands, and is extremely resist to onshore manufacturing. CEO repeatedly complained on CNBC that HP had built its supply chain in Asia over thirty years. HP can not build computers in US because all of the components are made in Asia.

If tariff is in place, by a strong Congress, the HP CEO will assemble a team to move back supply chain over night! Is CEO's job to complain about supply chain and do nothing? While CEO is paid in millions dollar, 74,000 HP workers in America have lost jobs. When Hewlett and Packard started business in 1939 at their garage, no engineers, no skilled workers, and no road map, but HP survived and thrived during the war. From 70s, HP successfully developed and commercialized calculators, printers, computers and servers. If HP has a will to move the mountains, it can rebuild supply chain in California!

A good example to onshore US manufacturing is done by Insulet, maker of insulin pump for diabetes patients. The company currently hires about 100 workers in its China factory to supply US markets. The company has planned to build second plants in Boston with equal capacity. In its new highly automated plant, Insulet will hire only 10 people to run entire factory. Robots and artificial intelligence management will massively improve productivity, improve supply chain efficiency, and reduce labor cost.

It will not be easy to pass legislation to raise tariff on imports, and to cut corporate tax. We face challenges of all kinds: betrayed politicians, pay-by-foreigners lobbyists, MNC with vested interests... Rebuilding American industry capacity will be very hard to materialize. When John Kennedy addressed 40,000 spectators at Rice University's stadium in Sep 1962, on the America's moon landing program, his famous speck still inspire and empower all Americans to put together a good fight.

"We choose to go to the moon. We choose to go to the moon in this decade and do the other things, not because they are easy, but because they are hard, because that goal will serve to organize and measure the best of our energies and skills, because that challenge is one that we are willing to accept, one we are unwilling to postpone, and one which we intend to win, and the others, too."

Chapter 3 - Balance Federal Budget To Save America From Bankruptcy

President Trump, Are you listening? Keep your campaign promises!

"For too long, a small group in our nation's capital has reaped the rewards of government while the people have borne the cost. Washington flourished, but the people did not share in its wealth. Politicians prospered, but the jobs left. And the factories closed.... And spent trillions and trillions of dollars overseas while America's infrastructure has fallen into disrepair and decay."

President Trump is absolutely right, Washington flourished and feasted during the worst financial crisis when jobs are gone, income are down for rest of Americans. In two year following crisis, Obama expanded employment at federal agency by 416,000. Between 2005 and 2010, the number of federal workers earning more than $150,000 soared 10 fold, and doubled in first two years of Obama. While millions in private sectors lost jobs, and many went offshore that would never returned, Washington had its best party during Obama time.

"The number of federal workers earning six-figure salaries has exploded during the recession, according to a USA TODAY analysis of federal salary data. Federal employees making salaries of $100,000 or more jumped from 14% to 19% of civil servants during the recession's first 18 months — and that's before overtime pay and bonuses are counted. Federal workers are enjoying an extraordinary boom time - in pay and hiring -

during a recession that has cost 7.3 million jobs in the private sector." (Dennis Cauchon)

After passing the $787 billion stimulus plan in 2009, Washington certainly "created" jobs! 4 of 5 of those were hired by federal agencies with the best pay and best benefit, plus pension, overtime pay, vacation. But, those positions not only do not produce any value, but also suffocate and regulate productive businesses of the nation. More jobs at the government, more burden on the society. Handout of fat government jobs to his friends and billion dollars "grants" to NGOs, Obama surely rewarded his voters. The nation is up for grab. Whoever has the dirty power, grab as much as they can.

On April 1, 2011, Stephen Moore of Wall Street Journal wrote an article that: "today in America, there are twice as many people working for the government (22.5 million) than in the all of manufacturing (11.5 million). This is an exact reversal of the situation in 1960, when there were 15 million worked in manufacturing, and 8.7 colleting a paycheck form the government."

The nation was changed by Obama, for the worse. Obama time was the darkest period in 240 years history of the republic: when free market was abandoned in favor of welfare, tax dollar was abused as special favors, free speech was censored by political correctness, racial discrimination become normal in the name of affirmative action.

A clear mind and a vote is a responsible citizen's weapon, use both wisely!

Our Federal Government Is Financial Broke

If a person stole $9 trillions tax money from the Treasury Department, and brought government to the edge of bankruptcy, is he the biggest financial criminal in American history?

That person is Barrack Hussein Obama.

During Obama's eight years, the nation debt skyrocketed to $19 trillion, from $10 trillion at the end of 2008. In 240 years history of the Republic, government accumulated $10 trillion debt, and Obama doubled the number in eight years! 2009 financial crisis was the perfect excuse for Obama to reward his voters with big fat "thank you" checks. As Obama's chief of Staff, Rahm Emanuel, said, "You never let a serious crisis go to waste. And what I mean by that it's an opportunity to do things you think you could not do before." Obama certainly did not "waste" the financial crisis: the 2009 budget deficit was 10% of GDP, another 9% deficit in 2010, 9% in 2011, and 7% in 2012.

The nation was outraged! TEA party protest erupted across the country in 2009 and 2010.

In eight year, Obama spent 5 dollar while government collected 3 dollar. From 1901 to 2010, 78 years out 110 years, our government was run on deficit, i.e. the government had to borrow money to pay for government programs, from military weaponry to federal employees, from SS to Medicare, from medical research to moon landing. But deficits were usually small. In 1929, total government budget was 3% of GDP; the year before World War II, 1942, total budget was 12% of GDP. Obama time: 24% of GDP

If entire government is shut down, while all tax revenue are collected to pay down debt, it will take 6 years. If the debt is allocated to each individual, every citizen has to shoulder $59,000 dollars!

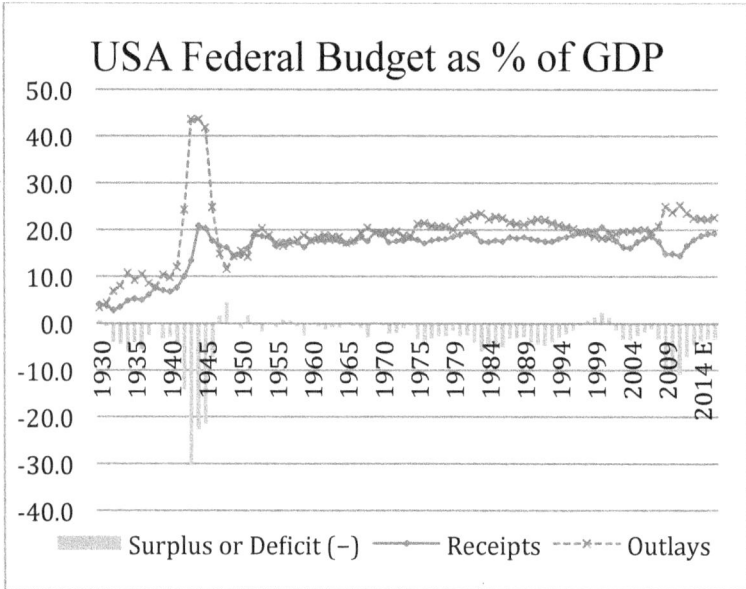

USA Federal Budget as % of GDP

Source: CBO, the White House

This astonishing, drunken-sailor spending has blown up debt ceiling year after year. Haircutting our budget spending apparently will not solve our debt problem. Deficit spending for decades has ruined national financial health, and our debt level has reached such a devastating level - only drastic and bold measures can restore our fiscal health.

The debt to American is like cancer to human body. Either we cut out the cancer, with decisiveness and will, bear the short-term pain to exchange for long-term health, or let the cancer grow and eat the body!

Damages have been done. With interest expense at $220 billion, it was already 6% of total government budget in 2012. Being the 4th biggest cost item, interest expense is next only to Defense, Medicare and Medicaid. If we stay on the path of deficit spending, by 2020, interest will reach $1 trillion, being the biggest cost in our national budget. Most of those interests are due to Chinese, Japanese, and mid-eastern countries. With less and less money, how can we afford defense, education, research, senior care, and social security? What is the future of America?

The nation not only cannot pay down its debt, but also can barely pay its interests!

There is really no way to reduce the debt without a revolution to blow away our social programs, and swept out those drunken, sold-out Congressmen. Even trimming defense spending and massive laying-off of agency workers, will not generate meaningful surplus to pay off debt. With an increasing debt burden, the Treasury can barely make ends meet. It does not sound popular to advocate budget cutting and fiscal austerity during a time of high unemployment and recession. Nevertheless, America needs a wakeup call now. America is financially broke!

Where did the money go? How could Obama waste $9 trillion in eight years and the Congress go with him?

Cause And Cure Of Federal Deficit

Obama's budget deficits were vastly wasted or stolen, including big checks to his voters and friends, and other old dues to entrenched interest groups.

Waste by military - The myth of Iraq war is not a conspiracy theory story, but a real accountability question that needs to be answered. Total spending on war in Iraq and Afghanistan estimated to be $3 trillion to $5 trillion dollars! Of course, they are all piled up on national debt that not single politicians cares out. What brought us to this huge waste of money and loss of life?

To revenge the 9/11 massacre? Those hijackers were all from Saudi! None of them from Iraq!

The iconized central banker, Alan Greenspan, in his memoir "*The Age of Turbulence: Adventures in a New World*" said that "I'm saddened that it is politically inconvenient to acknowledge what everyone knows: The Iraq war is largely about oil." But even him was dead wrong: on the bidding list for Iraq oil field post the war, there is No American oil company! America does not need Iraq oil!

"Those who claim that the U.S. invaded Iraq in 2003 to get control of the country's giant oil reserves will be left scratching their heads by the results of last weekend's auction of Iraqi oil contracts: Not a single U.S. company secured a deal in the auction of contracts that will shape the Iraqi oil industry for the next couple of decades. Two of the most lucrative of the multi-billion-dollar oil contracts went to two countries, which bitterly opposed the U.S. invasion — Russia and China.... won a bigger stake than the Americans in the most recent auction. " (Vivienne Walt, *Time*, Dec. 19, 2009)

America has been importing most oil from northern neighbor and southern neighbors. Because of obvious reasons, oil by pipeline and short ocean route were preferred over those mid-east oils. According to BP statistical review of world energy, 80% of US are from neighboring countries, only 20% from mid-eastern regions.

With ramp-up of shale gas and shale oil production, America is on its way of oil self-sufficiency! We do not need Iraq oil. Hence, what are our "vital interests" in the region? Why do we bother with those countries at all?

Even more ridiculous, why would America spending trillion defending Germany and rest of Europe, while Germany is the one of the richest country on earth, and running $200 billion trade surplus annually from us. Their advanced technology and wealth are more than sufficient to defend itself. Similarly, for Japan and South Korea, two countries being the 3rd and 12th largest economies, and trillion dollars trade surplus from us, they should pay very penny of cost for Americans to station in their country and defend their security!

Additionally, our spending on defense at $600 billion, is more than next 10 biggest countries combined, including China, Saudi Arabia, Russia, UK, India...Cold war was long over, and there is not major enemy threatening us. Why do we spend so much money on military? $100 million for a single F35? Chinese and Russians are making similar weapons at a small fraction of our cost!

With our nuclear arsenal in place, America is as safe as it can be. Yes, Americans wants to have strong defense, to safe guard our land, our people and democracy. But that safeguarding does not justify the massive military budget, does not justify Iraq war, does not justified spending of 20% of GDP!

Waste by Federal agencies - Democrat is the party of government - the bigger the government programs become, the more tax they can collect, the more successful the party is, and the more votes the party get. It is shocking how this party flourished when the rest of the world see America as the shining light of free market, as the strong hold of capitalism on earth. Inside America, the liberals had transformed America to a semi-communist nation, deprived productive citizens and brought the nation to the edge of bankruptcy.

The biggest enemy is often from inside!

U.S. Federal Spending – Fiscal Year 2010 ($ Billion)

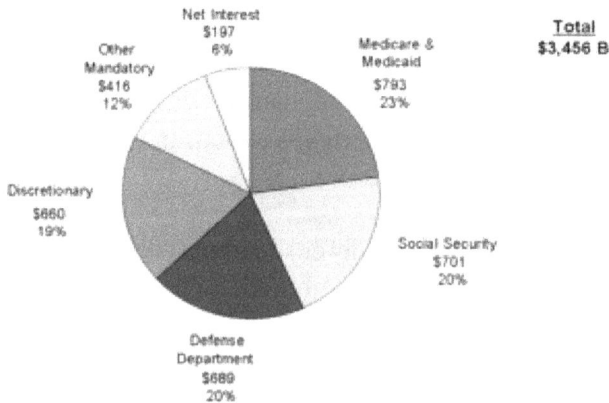

Net Interest
$197
6%

Other
Mandatory
$416
12%

Medicare &
Medicaid
$793
23%

Total
$3,456 B

Discretionary
$660
19%

Social Security
$701
20%

Defense
Department
$689
20%

Source Data: CBO Historical Tables

Source: CBO, the White House

To Democrats, the forever mantra is "tax tax, spend spend, elect and elect". Under Obama, we have more agency, more regulations, more budget, more tax, more spend, more deficit, and more debt. While cutting tax is welcomed, cutting government spending is not. Combined social security and Medicare accounts for 46% of federal budget, which is untouchable for both sides of Congress. Military spending is around 20% of GDP, which is vastly wasted and unnecessary.

While Democrats want to spend and Republicans want to cut, the only budget agreement both can sign on is borrowing, and more borrowing. Piling up on national debt, is the only solution year after year. No one cares about the future of America!

Waste on food stamps – It is astonishing how wasteful those government programs were, if not stolen. While the stimulus plan in 2009 were arguable and dubiously justifiable. The massive spending in following years by Obama was absolutely shocking and infuriating: food stamp at $77 billion a year for 44 million people?!

There is no starvation in America! Indeed, Americans are overeating and overweight, particularly among the population who rely on food stamp. In New York City, 1.7 million people are on food stamp (1 out 5 of people living there). Forty percent of public school kids in the city are overweight and those are the same kids living on food stamps.

The problem for the society is that Democrat's ever more spending are paid by tax from half of the population, while the other half are free riders. According to Tax Foundation, 97% of tax are paid by 49% of payers, and rest 51% of citizen pay 3%. Half of the wage earners do not pay a penny of tax! Those free riders, of course, always vote for Democrat, to get free food, free medicine, free education, and free....

The nation is divided, as deep as never before: divided on income and tax, divided on politics and social issues, divided on direction of the country, divided on heritage and connection with our past. The union is increasingly fragile. Can America still hold together?

This government is effective only for religious and moral people. America was built by people from Mayflower and similarly minded: the Christians who believed in hard working and perseverance, not welfares and entitlement. Building a new nation from scratch, no one handed them food, medicine, food stamp, Medicare, Medicaid, unemployment insurance, long-term disability, no privilege of any kind! Yet, the country survived civil war, Great Depression, 2 world war, cold war, and so on, and thrived on those hardships to become the world's superpower.

Democracy will not work when the nation lost its Christian values. When half America are permanent free riders, living on another half for food, housing, medicine, education, while share no value, no blood, no origin, no religion in common, who are those "deplorable" willing to pay for everything?

No, they are not.

They are angry and resentful to everything Obama has done to this country! They are tax-payers, serving in our army, hard working, ethical and religious "real Americans" who gathered under the Tea Party and Sara Palin, who voted Trump to White House. Trump victory is only a start of this revolution.

A new tax rebellion is not unthinkable. Remember that America revolution was a tax rebellion against Britain. And today's tax burden has reached its limit! It is only a matter of time for the TEA party movement to gain more supports to overthrow irresponsible Congress and lie-and-betray President!

It is a historical opportunity when Senate, House and White house are on the Right side, who believes in fiscal discipline, small government and low tax. If we cannot get tax burden aligning with political justice this time, we may never have a second chance before the debt eat our country!

Balanced Budget Amend should be in our Constitution! Without a Constitution amendment, debt ceiling has become a political gambling chip, not serving as the real constraint on debt offering. Although government was shut down numerous times, during Clinton and Obama, eventual compromises were reached and did not alter the path of continued debt binge, which is bankrupting America!

The only way to have a iron-fist rule to limit borrowing is to amend Constitution, as laid out by Rep. Tom Perriello (D-VA) on March 16, 2010, he said, "The only way to get Congress to balance the budget is to give them no choice. The only way to keep them out of the cookie jar is to give them no choice. Which is why, whether its balanced budget acts or pay as you go legislation or any of that -- it's the only thing. IF YOU DON'T TIE OUR HANDS, WE'LL KEEP STEALING."

The only way to "tie their hands" is to pass a balanced budget amendment of Constitution.

"In Trump We Trust" Ann Coulter enthusiastically titled her book to support Trump's campaign in 2016. Trump revolution provided a glimpse of hope to restore fiscal health and reduce debt, but that hope can wane away as politicians rarely held campaign promises to Americans.

Hence, it is every citizen's duty to remind Trump everyday: Keep your campaign promises!

CaliExit is not a bad idea, although it sounds horrific for the nation. Given how divided the society is, it might be a good solution. The ideology behind the division is deep and wide, and the chance of conciliation and union is very slim. Despite physical approximate, America is deeply separated into two societies: tax-payers and free-riders. For Democrats, their belief in entitlement of welfare, "fair" shot in equality of economic fruits, and taxation on the rich, is in sharp contrast of free market believers' small government, low tax, and traditional values (which are largely based on Christian traditions).

Christians believe in hard-working and perseverance in time of difficulty, and entitlement to fruits of their own work. Democrats want free food stamp, free education, free medicine, Medicare, Medicaid, social security, "equality" in income. Christians believe in "one god, one nation", but Democrat push God out of our classroom, and replace with consumerism, hedonism, secularism, multiculturalism, and degradation of the society. When God is out of classroom, and people out of Church, moral degradation is inevitable - teenagers of all colors have embraced alcohol, drug, crime and sex.

Without moral value and responsibility, students from public school are trained to be consumers and indulgers, not responsible citizens and unified Americans with ideals and dreams, like older generations.

Most importantly, the nation is divided two irreconcilable groups: tax payer and tax consumers. According to tax foundation, in 2014, 50% of wage earners paid almost no tax, while the other 50% paid 97% of total tax.

This is exactly what John Calhoun predicted in 150 years ago: "the necessary result, then of the unequal fiscal action of the government is, to divide the community into two great class; one consisting of those who, in reality, pay the taxes, and ...bear exclusively the burthen of supporting the government; and the other of those who are the recipient of their proceeds, through disbursements, and who are, in fact, supported by the government; or, in few words, to divide it into tax-payers and tax-consumers"

Let the Democrats secede to California and let Obama be the President of California. In the land of paradise, they can finally be "liberated" from free market and capitalistic America, and enjoy unprecedented:
- Free food stamp for all
- Free education
- Free medicine
- Free and equal housing
- Open border to immigration of all nations
- Open trade to all foreign goods
- Equality in income to all citizens!

How wonderful is this utopia communist California! All Democrats can move and live in California happily ever after. They can dance and party everyday, eat and drink for free with food stamp from Obama. They can pay same salary for everyone, and assign to same size of housing.

Is this what Obama dreamed of? Economic equality, regardless of race, gender, age, religion, education, origin...

The biggest challenge for this utopia is that no one pays tax! How can this new CaliExit provide free goodies when no one pays tax? The only way to organize this "free and equal" society is by dictatorship: forced labor and forced transfer! The dictator government agency decides what prices are (called planed central economy), and how labor results are distributed (equally), so that the Democrat can achieve equality for all.

"To impose an equality of rewards for unequal accomplishment is to nullify one of the goals of our Constitution – "to establish justice". It is to replace justice with injustice" (Patrick J. Buchanan, *Suicide of a Superpower)*

The utopia of communism had failed terribly under Lenin and Stalin in Russia, under Mao in China, under Jing in North Korea. The debate of how to achieve social equality has been long concluded, while communism as a social experiment has been dumped to trash bin. Unfortunately and dishearteningly, Obama was voted to White House to lead America on the "hopeless" road to equality.

All those welfares and benefits in America are paid by another half of population who shoulder tax burdens. They have every reason to be angry and upset by how tax money was wasted on ridiculous excuses, and how money was stolen by interest groups. Trillion dollars of debt was borrowed without a hint of responsibility.

Those diehard Democrats who voted for Obama, those 70 million who pays no tax, those 44 million food stamp collector, those 73 million on Medicaid, 24 million on government payroll, are welcome to secede California to build a communist utopia! Go ahead!

The future of CaliExit is called Venezuela. Actually they can merger in the future because they will be identical twins.

Keeping Social Security Status Quo Is Not An Option

Based on the 2010 social security trustee report, the trust fund currently holds assets of $2,540 billion. In 2009, the trust fund income was $807 billion, which were tax collected plus interest income. Currently, social security contribution is taxed at 12.4% as a payroll tax, equally split between employer and individual with a tax cap of $106,800. The benefits paid in 2009 were $686 billion.

On surface, social security seems all right based on the income statement, with income exceeding cost and with $2.5 trillion of assets. However, social security cost is projected to grow faster than social security income, particularly after 2015 because of demographic change, and consequently, social security trust fund will be depleted around year 2037.

The more depressing news is that the $2.5 trillion trust fund was "invested" in the special US Treasury bond. The trust fund did not invest in real assets such as stock or real estate, but in Treasury bonds, which were part of general government debt. Hence, those taxed money were already spent! There is no asset in the trust!

Indeed, social security trust is a Ponzi Scheme, with "saving" being spend by the government already, and future "return" has be paid with new money (tax) collected. In essence, social security is a transfer payment from younger generation to older ones, not a saving and insurance program.

Our government is already on $19 trillion debt. The real source of the future benefits is new social security tax to be collected. Current workers have to pay for those promised benefits to retirees and for their own benefits in future years.

Social security will go bankrupt regardless, only a matter of time. According to social security trustee, the fund asset is expected to diminish from 2025 and to be exhausted in 2037. Beyond 2037, the social security tax can only fulfill 75%-78% of promised benefits, without a hike of tax rate or tax base. If actuarial estimates are based on a more optimistic economic growth, the year of bankruptcy may be delayed till 2042. Regardless, social security cannot sustain.

Between 2011 and 2015, the imbalance between income and expenditure will be small, in years following 2015, as the population ages and more retirees collect their SS benefits, annual cost will significantly exceed income. The trust fund will quickly shrink after year 2025, and will be exhausted by 2037, under current tax and benefit schedule.

Social security and Medicare together eat 46% of federal spending in 2010. According to Congressional Budget Office, combined social security and Medicare cost will take 61% of federal budget in 2035. Entire country will be suffocated by the heavy burden of those spending! Where do we find money to pay for science and education, for military and investment?

America is on an economic suicide!

Medicare and Social Security Face Large Deficits

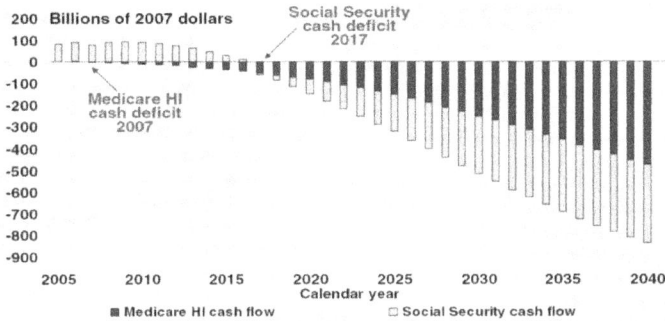

Source: GAO and SSA

To prevent the depletion of the trust fund and keep income and cost in balance, either payroll tax has to be increased or benefit has to be cut. While social security solvency can be calculated mathematically, in reality, the solution of increasing tax may not be feasible given overall tax burden. Any further increase in tax burden will be met with angry resistances. And of course, cutting benefits will anguish seniors.

Social security and Medicare, the most important benefits for seniors, are the untouchable "third rail of American politics". Populist and consensus rule is the mantra of today's politics - politicians do what the poll told them to do. There is no ideology principle. To gain votes in elections, politicians always over-promise the public what they will do once in office. Seniors' voters determine who will be the next President.

If a poll asks senior whether they like to have a paycheck every month, the answer is of course yes. But seniors do not have the responsibility of balance our national budget; do not have a sense of how disastrous national debt situation is and how it will be in the future. It is our elected politicians and Congress who should decide whether the society could afford those welfare programs.

Unfortunately, no politician has the courage to tell the truth to the public that America can not afford social security and Medicare. Instead, every President borrowed ever-more money and hiked tax to finance their pet programs: from social security, to Medicare, to public housing, free education, food stamps, minimum wages. As they hand out checks, politicians get elected and re-elected.

It is very much a legalized looting of the public wealth, whoever is in charge in Washington steals money from the public as much as they can. Politicians cater to the taste of the "perceived" majority, and majority loot from the minority whenever they have a chance. When there is nothing to loot, politicians borrow money. Politicians have no sense of responsibility for the US sovereign debt, because they are in office for only four years. It is the successor who has to deal with the debt, while the next politician in office thinks in the same way.

Should Social Security Exist At All?

The debated about social security has been ongoing since its inception. It was created under collectivism ideology that government should take care of citizens, which is fundamentally against the free market principle. The system was conceived during a time when economic condition was extremely distressed, and when demographics were totally different from it is today. Through numerous expansions, the program has become the second biggest spending program by the federal government. Given the deficit and debt level, American society can not afford all those welfare programs. Sooner or later, we have to abandon them, either by external force or internal conflict.

In 1935, when Social Security Act was passed, the tax burden was very modest. With a tax rate of 2% (split between employer and employee) at tax base of $3,000, the tax burden did not seem excessive. The tax rate was scheduled to reach 6% by 1950. Today, the upper threshold is $106,800, with tax rate of 12.4%.

When social security becomes fully operational in 1940, total cost of the social security was $35 million with beneficiaries of 222,488 people. In 2009, the spending skyrocketed to $615 billion with beneficiaries of 51 million people!

That is a typical scheme of government programs, with spending started small and finished big.

The number of people working versus the number of qualified beneficiary was 182 to 1 when first check was mailed out in 1940. That ratio decreased rapidly to 13 to 1 in 1950 and to 3.6 to 1 in 1960. In 2009, the ratio was 2.6 to 1.

Ratio of Employed Population versus Social Security Beneficiary

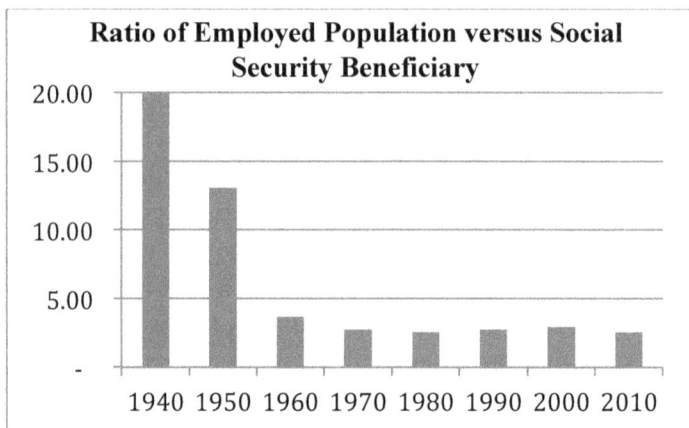

Source: SSA

More importantly, the life expectancy in 1935 was 61 years old. With social security beneficiary starting age of 65, most people did not even have a chance to claim a penny. Seventy years later, average life expectancy has reach 80s and for every 1 retiree, there are only 2.5 workers contributing to fund.

The demographic shift has made social security unsustainable and unfeasible! Face the reality!

Life Expectancy at Birth, by Sex in USA (in years)				
Year	Total	Male	Female	
1900-1902	49.2	47.9	50.7	
1909-1911	51.5	49.9	53.2	
1919-1921	56.4	55.5	57.4	
1929-1931	59.2	57.7	60.9	
1939-1941	63.6	61.6	65.9	
1949-1951	68.1	65.5	71	
1959-1961	69.9	66.8	73.2	
1969-1971	70.8	67	74.6	

1979-1981	73.9	70.1	77.6	
1989-1991	75.4	71.8	78.8	
2002	77.3	74.5	79.9	
2003	77.5	74.8	80.1	
Source: Congressional Research Service, US Census				

From 2013-2024, we can gradually phase out social security and Medicare while bringing budget into balance. Milton Friedman made excellent suggestions of replacing welfare programs with negative income tax in his 1980 bestseller *Free to Choose*. A negative income system will brilliantly end the New Deal trophy – social security - without adding new debt, tax and agency. Since it was proposed 30 years ago, negative income tax has drawn attentions from public and politicians. One day, it will become a reality.

From 2025-2036, after balancing budget and ending social security and Medicare, USA government can generate $1 trillion dollar budget surplus annually, so that it can reduce federal debt level to 20-30% of GDP at the end of period. To reduce national debt level to less than 20% of GDP in 20 years, annual surplus should be in 7-9% of GDP range. This may sound like a mission impossible, but does America have another option?

Balanced budget each and every year should be written into Constitution amendment, so that no politicians can find any excuse. This is the only way to restore the credibility of US government and of the Dollar. Of course, a dramatic change of economic relationship like this plan can easily cause social turmoil and unrest. Hence, ending social security and other welfare should be conducted on a gradual basis to provide enough time for recipients and payers to adjust. A decade may seem too long for an individual, but not for a nation to restore its taxation structure.

Abandoning welfare programs does not mean lack of concern for the poor and the elderly, or justification of unfair income distribution. Abandoning those programs will restore the free market efficiency and preserve individual rights. Social security and other welfare programs have not only distorted the role of a government for a free society, but also destroyed American values - reforming social security cannot do much help as the government is deeply in debt. It may require a generation people's hard work to pay down our national debt, to restore confidence and to revitalize American economy.

FDR Changed America' Path on Free Market

Great Depression was a turning point in American politic ideology. Before then, America society was essentially a free market system with a small government. Federal budgets were kept under 10% of national income for about 150 years since the independence. Under a political system that was invented for the first time in history with the power of government powers being checked and balanced, America prospered.

Great Depression was blamed as the failure of capitalism. Government stepped in to change social contracts, to re-distribute income, and to build welfare state. Combining public sentiment of the time and shrewd political maneuvers (such as nominating Justice of the Supreme Court), Democratic Party became the dominant power in decades following Great Depression. From 1860 to 1932, Republican held Presidency in 66 out of 72 years. From 1932 to 1980, Democrats held Presidency 32 out of 48 years. In Congress, the power was shifted to the Liberal side as well. From 1935 to 1965, Democrats controlled both the House and Senate for 26 out of 30 years.

The ideology of the Liberals to create equal society resulted in high taxation, big government and big spending. After FDR was sworn into office in 1933, government spending as percentage of GDP has been on an every-rising spiral, climbing from 3.4% in 1930, to 20-25% in recent years (42% during World War II). While war spending was excusable and temporary, the expansions of government during peace time were mostly due to establishment of welfare programs, including poverty assistance, food stamp, free education, housing subsidies, SS and Medicare. From 1930, government has been running on deficit in 67 out of 80 years.

Is it necessary and beneficiary to expand the size and function of government? Government size (measured as budget/GDP) has trended up in last few hundreds years in almost every many countries, regardless of dominant societal ideology, development stage, and social system. Was the increase caused by the complexity of governing a modern society? Or by the desire and power of politicians?

Of the essential functions of a government, no one summarized better than Adam Smith in 1776. "According to the system of natural liberty, the sovereign has only three duties to attend to; three duties of great importance, indeed, but plain and intelligible to common understandings: first, the duty of protecting the society from violence and invasion of other independent societies; secondly, the duty of protecting, as far as possible, every member of the society from the injustice or oppression of every other member of it, or the duty of establishing an exact administration of justice; and, thirdly, the duty of erecting and maintaining certain public works and certain public institutions which it can never be for the interest of any individual, or small number of individuals, to erect and maintain; because the profit could never repay the expense to any individual or small number of individuals, though it may frequently do much more than repay it to a great society."

A man in a free society is essential left alone to do whatever he likes. He pursues his happiness, engages his business, and trades voluntarily with other members of the society. No force is allowed in a free society, except forces by criminal and government. If the society is threatened by constant violence, from either outside or inside forces, no man can engage in productive activities, such as manufacturing, agriculture, and service. Man in an uncivilized society has to be armed and defend himself and his family.

The evolution of human society and job specialization rendered it possible to establish an organized society that a man can have a productive job without worrying being robbed. After industrialization, productivity gain and job specialization reached an unprecedented new level with men freed from agricultural activities. They moved to cities, worked in factories, created new technologies, and established new business. They were free and, owned their properties and productions. No longer was the case that man had to work for their landlord on farming, where they had no ownership in the means of production and in the result of production. They were not enslaved by anyone, not even their king or government.

This was a very new social phenomenon that started few hundreds years ago. During most part of recorded human history, people were either enslaved, without ownership of their life, or exploited, without ownership of their production. Ownership of life is the first thing a free person desires.

Nature did not entitle human being with powerful claws and strong teeth. Food did not come easy for human to survive on earth. Man had to learn, think, and judge, when he grew crops or catch fishes. <u>Man was entitled to nothing on the earth except what he produced.</u> After acquiring skills to produce, man started to enjoy delicacy food, warm clothes and good houses.

However, for most of the time in history, only small percentage of human were able to enjoy the result of production, while majority of man lived and worked for others by force. Only after Renaissance and, particularly after Industrial Revolution, man were finally freed from social chains – they are free to decide where they like to live and work, free to choose a profession, free to trade with other voluntarily, without being forced or dictated.

In a free society, the law, free from intrusions of other man, protects man's rights to life and properties. There are trespasses and violations from time to time, which necessitate for government to be the judge once disputes happen. The court of law exists to fulfill the function.

Government was established to intermediate men of the society so that man benefit from living in a civilized society by exchanging knowledge and trading goods. Otherwise, living on an island would be perfectly ideal. Law is to protect individual from the government, and from other violators. Because government is the only legalized force, man is under constant threat of being violated by his government. Limiting the power of the government is a top priority for a free society.

Founding fathers knew all those too well by observing what happened in entire human history. American government was limited in power and in size from the very beginning, which three branches were in check and balance. During first 150 years of American history, government was granted with the power that was explicitly permitted by the people. Business was left alone with minimal interventions from the government. In a laissez faire free market, America prospered and thrived.

Great Depression turned the direction and changed the society. Great Depression was viewed as the prove of failure of capitalism and free market, while the government and central bank indeed plotted and caused the entire disaster. With control of the mass media, government smeared private business as the culprit of Great Depression, and as the cause of hardship, greed, bad work condition, low salary, ruthless competition, and lack of care of workers. Welfare and central planning was promoted to be the solution for unemployment and economic recovery. FDR's advisors and intellectuals were eager to promote social fairness and government responsibility. They also borrowed from the experience of welfare state in Germany, England and Sweden. During Roosevelt time and following decades, Democrats were all out building welfare state – Great Society, in America. And the nation was on a wrong direction until... Reagan revolution.

Building Welfare State in America

"Iron Chancellor" Bismarck created early example of modern welfare state. In 1880s, his cabinet passed a series of social insurance program to cover old age, accident, medical and unemployment. It may seem strange to us today why an authoritarian, right wing German dictator was concerned of social welfare, which is generally linked to socialism and the left. According to Bismarck, "The great questions of the time will not be resolved by speeches and majority decisions—that was the great mistake of 1848 and 1849—but by iron and blood."

However, examined in detail, it would be no surprise that Bismarck and socialist shared common believing in command economy. Ruling class in both systems promoted "public interest" as the noble goal for citizen to sacrifice. Their paternalistic concern for lower class was to demonstrate ruling class' superiority. Ruling elite believed that they knew how to take care of the public than the public themselves. In both systems, government was the ruler of the society, not servants of the public. Building welfare programs for the public give them a God-like feeling. Also, Bismarck's social insurance was motivated by shrewd politics to defend socialist movement and to win support of industry.

In early 20th centuries, Britain and Sweden also adopted similar social insurance and welfare programs to promote equality of opportunity, equitable distribution of wealth, and public responsibility. Through World War II, welfare state building reached a new level that extended further to 60s.

Great Depression changed American attitude to welfare state. While mutual insurance to help each other in case of disability and unemployment had existed in trade union for decades, a universal, social insurance was still new to America, and was indeed was against laissez faire principle deeply entrenched in America. FDR grasped the historical opportunity and expanded government's role into new territories.

With unemployment hovered around 25% in 1932, the influence of business reached its bottom. FDR overwhelmingly won the 1932 election with Democratic majority in the Congress. During his first 100 days, FDR passed numerous legislations that changed the economic structure of the society. Of those that survived till today would include SEC, FDIC, Social Security. Because of his early career in insurance industry, FDR was very familiar with the scheme of setting up insurance program. To make the social security acceptable to the Congress, he designed a contributory tax and benefit system that looked like insurance and pension plan, but being neither.

For insurances plans, buyers contribute premium to the pool of money, the trust fund. In case of accident, such as car accident, the buyer will be compensated for the loss. Because it is unlikely for all buyers to occur accidents, the pooled money in trust fund is enough cover incidents happened to small portion of plan participants. In case premium exceeds cost, the trust fund will accumulate assets for future events. Social security is not an insurance plan because every participant will retire and claim benefits. It is almost for certain from the very beginning that

Social security would not be sustainable unless the benefit is small and tax is high.

For retirement plan, individual accounts are set up to save and invest, in both defined benefit plan and defined contribution plan. Social security is not a retirement plan because money is pooled and re-distributed. The so-called conservative investment of SS fund is literally a Ponzi scheme because the entire fund is invested in special government bond. Government borrowed all saved money in trust fund and spend as if they are part of general budget. If the fund had invested in stock markets or bank loans or mortgage securities, it would be credible to believe that the Social security surpluses have been invested.

However, because government is the Social security investment manager and the borrower of the money in Social security trust fund, Social security plan fits every criteria of being a Ponzi Scheme – in which case a fund manager use newly attracted money to pay off existing clients by telling them the fund manager generated positive returns. The Social security surplus money was lend to the Dept. of Treasury and has been looted. Future Social security benefits can only be paid by new taxations. Who would accept Treasury notes as monthly check?

Social security Trust fund does not really exist! The $2.5 trillion trust fund holds only IOU promises from the government, which owes $14 trillion of debt already.

Social security was ingeniously designed to buy votes from seniors. It is neither insurance nor retirement plan. If the surplus had invested in stock markets, the financial health of the program would be much stronger. Unfortunately, shrewd politicians cheated public by calling the program contributory retirement plan when actually the money has been exchanged with IOU notes from the government. Any benefit money issued in the future can not be Treasury bills; therefore, only new taxation will solve the problem of short funding.

Essentially, Social security is a transfer of income from employed worker to retirees, by forced taxation on millions and with an illusion of security and insurance. It is taxed regressively because it is a flat taxation on employees and employers alike to a wage cap. A 6.2% tax up to 100. It is also distributed regressively, although has been modified numerous times. SS program has been expanded numerous times. The most significant happened in 1983 when President Reagan directed Alan Greenspan to study and make recommendations of reforming SS. The Greenspan committee suggested hiking tax rate and tax cap to bring SS from near bankruptcy to surplus.

By designing and administrating the program, government gained the image of taking care of the old and the sick, a God-like ruler, when the society lost as a whole by paying the program twice.

In response to criticism of Social security, Roosevelt: "I guess you're (Luther Gulick) right on the economics, but those taxes were never a problem of economics. They are politics all the way through. We put those payroll contributions there so as to give the contributors a legal, moral, and political right to collect their pensions and their unemployment benefits. With those taxes in there, no damn politician can ever scrap my social security program."

Chapter 4 - Phase Out Social Security And Medicare

Nov. 11, 1620, Mayflower anchored on Cape Cod, after a rough journey to cross Atlantic Ocean from Plymouth, England. 102 people onboard the ship dreamed a place that they can practice their religion without being persecuted. As Alice Bradford, the wife of William Bradford, the first governor of this group of settlers, found that they were "surrounded on all sides by this vast wilderness, was a little town, the very beginnings of Christian civilization out in the wilderness, and I thought, here we can do God's work."

The first winter was particularly harsh and brutal after Mayflower pilgrims settled in new world. What greeted them was disease, snow, and wild jungle, half of them died during the winter.

That was the starting for millions immigrant in the new world: no hospital, no housing, no food, and no charity. Everyone worked with their hands and brains, and only entitlements were their own products.

Men coming to earth were entitled to nothing except their own work. Actually, they were deprived of their own work in most time of history. Only in recent few hundreds years, men were finally freed and had full claim to their own work, and able to trade with others as they wish to.

Each free man trades his goods with others at a mutually agreed up price. This simple, straightforward, and fair system was later called free market capitalism. Upon this foundation, people built a thriving, prosperous and powerful America.

Four hundreds years later, entitlements are eating the republic away. The principle founding fathers had fight with their lives, free market capitalism, is now under grievous threats.

Who Is Paying Your Medical Bills?

The relationship between buyer and seller can be best illustrated by a matrix (Milton Friedman, *Free to Choose, A Personal Statement*). Basically, there are four types of buyer-seller relationship: Type I, II, III and IV. In type I transactions, you spend money on yourself. As you are using your own money to exchange voluntarily with a seller, you are motivated to maximizing your own economic interests by negotiating price and finding the best value. This type of transaction is what free market favors and what creates the economic efficiency.

In type II transaction, you are spending money on someone else, such as buying a gift for a friend. You are spending out of pocket and hence, are as cost-cautious as you are in type I. You are interested in finding the best value your friend likes.

In type III, someone else spends money on you, for example, a lunch on a corporate account. You have no incentive to keep the cost down. In this case, you are still interested in getting the best value on the market place, although someone else is paying for it.

In type IV, you are spending someone else's money on someone else. You have no incentive to keep the cost down and no incentive to find the best value. In this situation, you are simply an administrator for the transaction, and a disinterested buyer on the market according to rules given by the true buyers.

Recipient of Benefit

		You	Someone Else
Source of Money	You	I	II
	Someone Else	III	IV

Most welfare programs belong to the Type IV transaction with government agencies acting as the buyer for the welfare recipients. The agency has no incentive to control costs because money is from faceless "tax payer" and the administrator of the program is simply a pass-through. The administrator did not receive the good or service either, therefore, is not concerned of quality of the purchase. Like other third-party payer system, welfare programs create waste and inefficiency.

The fundamental flaw of the government administrated Medicare and Medicaid program lies in being the type IV transaction. The agency running the program, CMS (Center for Medicare Service), and SSA (Social Security Administration) spends taxpayers' money on another group of taxpayers. When medical or payment bills come to the desk, the agency simple writes checks on demand. Under this system, it is inevitable to see abuse, fraud, and corruption, in addition to waste and inefficiency.

One justification for socialized medicine is that medical services are too expensive and become unaffordable, particular for the low income and elderly. Like many other good-will welfare programs, they are distorted and abused once being implemented. Socialized medicine was intended to alleviate the heavy medical burdens. Nevertheless, this justification for Medicare cannot be further from the truth. No evidence supports that a government run healthcare program is cheaper and more affordable for the society than a private equivalent.

Government officials running Medicare program always have motives and justifications to expand the program and spend more money because existing services are "inadequate" for seniors. By expanding the program, those officials secure employment for themselves by controlling more spending. More spending means more tax and more power.

Milton Friedman commented in 1991 that a "casual glance at input and output in U.S. hospitals indicate that Gammon's law has been in full operation in the US since the end of WW II and especially since the enactment of Medicare and Medicaid in 1965".

"Before 1940, input and output both rose, input somewhat more than output, presumably because of the introduction of more sophisticated and expensive treatment. The cost of hospital care per resident of the U.S., adjusted for inflation, rose at the rate of 5% per year from 1929 to 1940; the number of occupied beds, at 2.4% a year. Cost per patient day, adjusted for inflation, rose only modestly."

"The situation was very different after the war. From 1946 to 1989, the number of beds per 1,000 population fell by more than one-half; the occupancy rate, by one-eighth. In sharp contrast, input skyrocketed. Hospital personnel per occupied bed multiplied nearly seven-fold and cost per patient day, adjusted for inflation, an astounding 26-fold. One major engine of these changes was the enactment of Medicare and Medicaid in 1965. A mild rise in input was turned into a meteoric rise; a mild fall in output, into a rapid decline."

From Social Security to Medicare

It took thirty years with a long, winding path to conceive, design and pass Medicare. The initial social security act included a paragraph about providing medical service to seniors, but the item was deleted by FDR due to fear that the bill would not pass if medical care was included. Following the pass of social security, the Left continued their effort to socialize medical service so that all the people could have equitable access regardless of their income. Equality is Liberals' forever goal.

Winning World War II significantly strengthened the Liberal's ideology that state control and central command is the way American society should be run. Socialization and entitled access to job, food, housing, medical care, pension and education become the goal of the Liberals. Those thoughts were reflected in Bill of Economic Rights and renewed New Deal progression, which were temporarily interrupted by the World War II.

Truman took over the effort to pass a universal health insurance in early 1950s. Truman said in 1948 State of the Union address that his goal was "to enact a comprehensive insurance system which would remove the money barrier between illness and therapy, protect all our people equally against ill health."

Yet, universal health insurance did not gain enough support despite that Democrats controlled both houses of the Congress in 1940s and 1950s. Facing congressional reluctance, Truman's advisors changed the goal of universal health coverage to those aged over 65 who contributed to the social security during employment, and the program was called Medicare. The bill did not fully cover seniors' medical needs, but instead focused on insuring hospital expenses, and later-on added physician fees, but left out of drug benefits. This was a quite peculiar, complex medical plan with coverage holes for a special age group.

After initial proposal of Medicare plan in 1952, the idea gradually gained momentum in Congress and political support from interest groups. From 1958 to 1965, congressional finance committee held annual hearings on the Medicare bill. Those hearings became heated battle ground for interest groups from both sides. While labor union and retirees were on the pro side of the bill, American Medical Association (AMA, Blue Shields, and conservatives were against it. AMA, representing medical professionals, believed that Medicare program was not "only unnecessary, but also dangerous to the basic principle underlying our American system of medical care"

Unlike many European countries' medical plans that started with coverage of low-income group and expanded to general populations, America health socialization started with coverage of aged ones. Using low-income method requires means tests, which is loathed by Republican legislators. To design a healthcare program that avoids means test and general coverage, the aged group became a natural selection to start with. Because this group earned relative low income, consumed most of healthcare resources, and commanded public sympathy, political opponents of Medicare found it hard to reject. Nevertheless, opponents succeeded in limiting the scope of Medicare plan.

Source: the White House. FDR and Lyndon Johnson in 1935.

After winning Presidential election over Barry Goldwater, Lyndon Johnson, with his unshakable commitment and political savvy, was all ready to pass a Medicare plan. Even though Democrats controlled both houses of Congress, Johnson proceeded with caution. At the end, Medicare, a social health insurance plan for American elderly, was finally signed into law as amendments to social security act on July 30, 1965. And first enrollee of Medicare was former President Truman and his wife Bess.

There was no guiding principle in Medicare plan. It was quite different from health programs legislated in European countries prior to an American version, reflecting both ideological bias and political reality. The program itself is a compromise between those who strongly advocate socialized medicine, similar to UK's National Health Service, and those who are against any governmental interventions.

There was a clear mismatch of what Medicare covers, and what seniors need. It is mostly an insurance plan for catastrophic events, i.e. hospital expenses in case of severe illness, not a socialized medicine or comprehensive medical coverage. Those who advocated socialized medicine compromised the program as a step stone for a broad, universal coverage with equitable access for all, while the cost shared among rich and poor, young and old.

It was very difficult for the conservatives to reject a program that provides care to seniors who have the advantage of emotional support from the public and have the voting power. In essence, Medicare is one additional way to re-distribute income. In 2006, Medicare was expanded to cover prescription drugs for seniors.

In retrospect of progressive legislation of Social Security and Medicare, Norman Thomas's prediction was shockingly prophetic: "The American people will never knowingly adopt socialism, but under the name of liberalism they will adopt every fragment of the socialist program until one day America will be a socialist nation without ever knowing how it happened." (Norman Thomas, 1884-1968, American socialist)

Fortunately, the expansion of Medicare has been slow, and disappointed Liberals who had hoped to expand the coverage to the general population much sooner. The main expansion of Medicare, the Part D covering drugs, did not happen until forty years after initial Medicare plan. The reality reflected American's general distrust of government run healthcare plans, after witnessing the failure of socialized medicine in UK and other European countries.

Source: AMA record album, "Ronald Reagan Speaks Out Against Socialized Medicine"

Reagan stated in the 1961 AMA recording about stopping Medicare that: "If you don't and I don't do it, one of these days you and I are going to spend our sunset years telling our children and our children's children what it once was like in America when men were free." Reagan warned that if Americans did not stop the proposed Medicare, "behind it will come other government programs that will invade every area of freedom as we have known it in this country until one day as Norman Thomas said we will wake to find that we have socialism."

Medicare Costs Are Unbearable

In 2010, total spending of Medicare reached $523 billion, equivalent to 3.6% of GDP. The number of beneficiary was 47.5 million. A modest small healthcare program for senior citizen has grown into a national unbearable burden. In 1970, the program covered 20 million elderly with spending of $7.5 billion. While the enrollment doubled (2.4x times), cost has risen 70x times. Even if the projection of future cost includes various cost containment legislation, Medicare spending is forecast to rise from 3.6% of GDP in 2010 to 6.2% in 2085.

The combined cost of Social Security and Medical will consume 12.2% of GDP in 2085. These two programs will cripple the government and destroy the country's future because they will consume 63% of federal budget in 2085 (rising from 43% in 2010). If cost containment legislations currently pending at Congress fail, and cost trend of Social Security and Medicare continues, these two programs may spend up to 79% of federal budget.

When a government spends majority of tax revenue on pension and medical bills, how can the country strengthen military, improve education, invest and increase productivity? Without a strong economy and technological advancement, what is the future of America? Instead of focusing on economic growth and building national strength, our government is occupied by busy administration of pension and medical services! Those behaviors are suicidal.

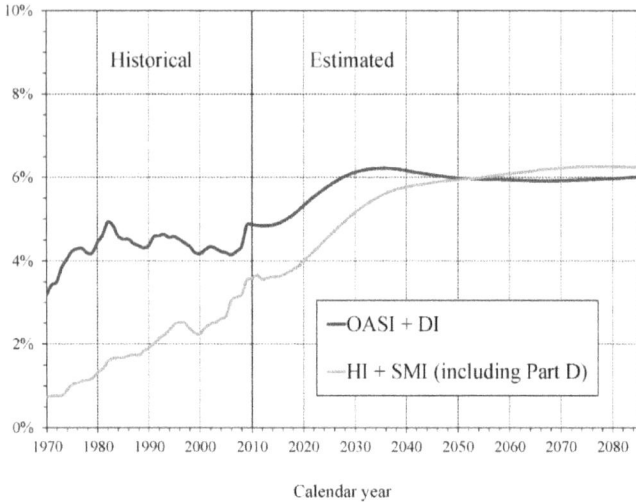

Calendar year

Source: CBO and SSA

The Medicare trust fund, like Social Security trust fund, will be
exhausted around 2030, plus/minus several years. The real
concern is more than about exhaustion of the trust fund, it is
about tax burden on the people. Because of the design of
Medicare financing and demographic change, cost growth will far
exceed GDP growth in following decades. The crisis can be
solved only by increasing tax or reducing benefits. Is the society
willing to bear more tax? The rise of TEA party had answered
the question clearly and loudly: no, Taxed Enough Already!

The intriguing tax scheme of the program created illusion that
people contribute to the own benefit, "give the contributors a
legal, moral, and political right to collect their pensions and their
unemployment benefits. With those taxes in there, no damn
politician can ever scrap my social security program." (FDR)
However, in essence, the program is a forced transfer of payment
from young to old. Using legalized forces to transfer income

between different groups of people should NOT be in the power of the government. It is an individual's most fundamental right to possess his/her production (in monetary form). Only a criminal or a government can violate the right by using forces and taking money away from a person.

Nevertheless, politicians use public's sympathy and tricky tax schedule to coerce people accepting those taxations so that politicians have more money to spend on their favored interest groups and to reward political supporters, all in the name of helping the elderly and the poor.

Medical cost will exceed the program's income from 2011 to 2085, with exception of few years. The fundamental reason for rising cost is the relationship between doctor-patient in Medicare, i.e. Type IV transaction. With a government payer as wedge between doctor-patient, no one has concern for cost because money is from the pool of common interest. More treatments and tests mean making more money for doctors. Consequently, outpatient becomes inpatient, short stay becomes long stay. Under this economic relation, medical costs went wild.

Facing the skyrocketing medical costs and in a helpless despair, in 1983, the government resorted to the last straw to contain Medicare cost – a fixed pay for a specific treatment under a system called Diagnosis-related group (DRG). Instead of reimbursing doctors what they charged in treating Medicare patients, the new prospective system paid doctors on a predetermined fee based on the patient's disease. This is quite shockingly for Reagan Administration to implement a price-fixing system by government, rather a market based pricing. It contradicted with Reagan's fundamental economic philosophy, free market capitalism. From the beginning, Reagan fought hard against Medicare.

Implementing DRG demonstrated how severely out-of-control were Medicare costs during 1970s. DRG is an extremely complicated reimbursement system with thousands pages of coding and regulations. Administrating DRG requires tremendous government resources and budget, when the government is already in deep debt and in deficit. While Medicare being complained by all sides of participants, doctors, patients, tax payers, why did the government trouble itself with creating and implementing this unnecessary, inefficient, unwelcome healthcare program? A complicated payment system is subject to cheating and abusing, and Medicare certainly has been abused.

"GAO has designated Medicare as a high-risk program since 1990, in part because the program's size and complexity make it vulnerable to fraud, waste, and abuse." (Kathleen M. King, Director, Health Care team at U.S. Government Accountability Office)

As a Type IV transaction, Medicare replaced the direct patient-doctor relationship with patient-payer-doctor. Not surprisingly, payer of the system has no knowledge of what was delivered at point of care. Doctors charged CMS for the service into a computer system and were paid by CMS. Patients received the care for free (except co-pay and deductible, but most are paid by CMS). The vulnerability of the system is that the payer is a faceless government. Patients received the care has limited choice, and limited knowledge of what they should get for the money. Because patients already paid tax and contributed to the system, they believe they deserve the best available care; and if they do not use the service, someone else will.

Doctors are incentivized to over-treat the patients because government is paying for everything and doctors are rewarded financially as well. Even if a procedure can be done on an outpatient basis, the doctor would like to prescribe a hospital stay with few days of recovery and observation. In the end, since cost is no issue, why should they bother?

Not only the system encourages more treatment than necessary, but also it can be abused. For example, doctors can bill CMS for services, procedures, supplies that were not provided. Or:
- Provide unnecessary services or unnecessary diagnosis.
- Misrepresent what was provided, when it was provided, and identity of the patient.
- Charge twice for the same service.
- Upgrade the coding in the CMS system for a service that reimburses more.

Those abuses and frauds are brazen and shocking to observers. For examples:

- In early 2010, Medicare paid $135,000 to a discount pharmacy in Hialeah, Fla. for drug prescriptions written by four doctors. First, two of the doctors were dead. A third doctor was alive, living in Portland, Ore., but he never wrote the prescriptions. The fourth doctor was a few months into a three-year prison sentence, according to federal court records, for conspiracy to commit Medicare fraud. (Source: Jim Kouri, Law Enforcement Examiner, July 23, 2009)
- In Florida, a dermatologist was sentenced to 22 years in prison, paid $3.7 million in restitution, forfeited an addition $3.7 million, and paid a $25,000 fine for performing 3,086 medically unnecessary surgeries on 865 Medicare beneficiaries. (Source: U.S. Department of Health and Human Services and Department of Justice.

*Health Care Fraud and Abuse Control Program Annual
Report for FY 2007* (2008)

- Dentists like Dr. Dolly Rosen, who within 12 months
  somehow built the state's biggest Medicaid dental practice
  out of a Brooklyn storefront, where she claimed to have
  performed as many as 991 procedures a day in 2003....
  Medicaid has even drawn several criminal rings that
  duped the program into paying for an expensive muscle-
  building drug intended for AIDS patients that was then
  diverted to bodybuilders. The cost of the drug was $6,400
  a month. A single doctor in Brooklyn prescribed $11.5
  million worth of the drug (Source: The New York Times,
  July 18, 2005 By CLIFFORD J. LEVY and MICHAEL
  LUO)

The United States Government Accountability Office (GAO)
estimated that $1 out of every $7 spent on Medicare is lost to
fraud and abuse. In 1998 alone, Medicare might lose nearly $12
billion to fraudulent or unnecessary claims. Real loss can only be
higher than the number from government's own estimates. Fraud
within the program contributes to the program's cost by an
estimated $60 billion a year, according to estimates by The
Center for Public Integrity in 2011. Total Medicare spending in
2010 was $522 billion.

Socialized Medicine in Britain

Proponents of socialized medicine, compromised to accept
Medicare and wished to expand the program later years, often
cited the "successful" system in Britain, Canada and even
Belgium, as role model. National Health System (NHS) of UK
was credited and well admired by the Liberals. Michael Moore's
2007 movie *Sicko* voiced the Liberals' ideals and wishes in
universal healthcare coverage.

What really happened in this free, noble and universal healthcare
system?

All British citizen and legal residents are treated free at the point
of service based on medical needs, not affordability. Nearly
entire medical professionals are government employees, paid by
general tax revenue. The system controls how doctors conduct
their work, and restrict their working hours, salaries, and
available drugs. The direct patient-doctor relationship lasted for
200 years in Britain was entirely abandoned. The claimed "moral
leadership" system caused "brain drain" of medical professionals
from UK. Through 1970s, near 1/3 of physicians graduated from
medical universities emigrated each year. While the expenditure
on program increased in 10 folds in sixty years, output measured
in various matrixes decreased significantly during the period.
Doctors fled the countries and people waiting for hospital beds
and surgeries reached near one million in any given year.

On The New York Times, Feb 12, 1964, " Prof. Ian Bush and his
research team are leaving Birmingham University for the
Worcester Foundation for Experimental Biology in Shrewsbury,
Mass. ... Professor Bush's decision was term "tragic" by Sir
George Pickering. President of the British Medical Association.

He describe the professor as the most brilliant pupil I ever had and one of the most brilliant people I have ever met"

Again on Feb 16, "in the last academic year, Britain lost 160 senior university teachers, about 60 of them to the US, according to a survey published by the Association of University Teachers...British scientists with newly acquired Ph.D. have been leaving the country permanently at a rate of at least 140 a year, according to a report last year by the Royal Society. This would be about 12% of the nation's output"

Dr. Max Gammon, a British physician who researched NHS, created "the theory of bureaucratic displacement" (Gammon's Law), under which "increase in expenditure will be matched by a fall in production." He observed in 2005 that: "When the NHS was established in 1948 we had 480,000 hospital beds. By the year 2000 the number had fallen to 186,000. This represents a fall from 10 beds for every thousand of the population in 1948 to 3.7 in the year 2000."

"As for staff, the number employed by the NHS has more than doubled from 350,000 in 1948 to 882,000 in 2002. The greatest percentage increase has been among designated administrative staff. Between 1997 and 2002 Senior Managers and Managers increased by no less than **47.6%** compared to an overall increase in the workforce of **16%** (nurses increased by **1.8%**)"

Phase out Social Security and Medicare – wrong concept and wrong ideology

The best and easiest fix of the Medicare is abandoning the program. It is wrong philosophically by permitting government to dictate what happens in a doctor's room. It is wrong economically by encouraging waste and abuse and causing gigantic financial burden on the society. Welfare medical care changes the direct buyer-seller relationship between doctor and patient. And more importantly, it misleads public into a wrongful dependence on the government from cradle to grave.

Medicare can be abandoned immediately by switching patients into a voucher system or private insurance scheme so that people have time to adjust. Negative income tax can be simultaneously implemented to help the poor with medical misfortunes. The long struggle of controlling medical cost, seemingly unwinnable, can be taken away from the bureaucrats' hands and be determined by the market.

The fundamental flaw of social security lies in its concept, which is the forced transfer of income in the disguise of saving and insurance scheme. It is neither a retirement and nor a insurance program, rather it is a special tax that transfers income from young, working people to old, retired population.

Transferring of income is a direct violation of individual rights. The government should be not given the responsibility of dictating how people should support their elderly. Social security also expands government's function beyond what Adam Smith prescribed. By expanding welfare program and deficit spending, the government grabbed power from the people and became an ever more inefficient, sloppy, and self-important bureaucracy. Government also has the monopoly of using legalize force to exert taxation from all members. Under the disguise of helping the poor, the old, and the less privileged, which sounds noble and kind, government forced transfer of income from more productive members of the society to less productive ones. Using well-disguised kindness and promises, politicians stole money and power from the public.

Ironically, family value is destroyed, not enhanced, by forced social security tax, because social security dictates how shall we support parents and grandparents. As government intrudes American families, social security reduces the sense of responsibility, while encourages reliance on the government. For thousands years of history, it is very usual for people to take care of parents and grand parents financially. Mutual support, care and love keep family together. Social security alienates family members by outsourcing financial support to the government while politicians take the role. By pretending having a heart for the old and the poor, politicians become the ruler, and gain them a god-like status.

By establishing welfare state, government becomes a caregiver that provides retirement, healthcare, education, and insurance and even entertainment. Public become child like dependents, relying on government from "cradle to grave". Those responsibilities saddle government agencies with administrative nuances and inefficiencies. Abandoning social security will relieve the government from the heavy burden of being a security provider and care giver, and will encourage saving and enhance family value, which is the foundation of American society, and more importantly, will help balance national budget and reduce debt level.

Social security is a vote-buying scheme by politicians, who promise the public of favors during election and pay off those voters by rewarding them with benefits, tax rebates and refunds etc. using deficit spending and debt borrowing. The repeated "debt is tomorrow's problem" political games have ruined the nation's financial health and destroyed Founding Fathers' principles. Washington becomes a gang-ruled place without ideology. Whoever has the force will steal whatever they can from the society, by a process called "legislation". Majority rule is not democracy, but gang rule.

From FDR to Lyndon Johnson, American has been lost in a mixed ideology, and lost her missions and ideals. As American gave up its faith in free market and individual freedom, government has expanded in every possible ways to take away people's rights - with the claim of helping the old and the poor.

In decades following the pass of 1935 social security Act, the welfare state and collectivism furthered the march into individual right and freedom. World War II justified the Liberal's claim that central planning and government control was the way to run America and to manage its economy. During the war, government took total control of the means and results of production. There is no doubt that American mighty industrial prowess and weaponry production overwhelmingly triumphed over enemies.

Unfortunately wartime success became the excuse for government to expand its role in managing the people and economy during peace time. More welfare programs and bigger federal budget deficit than ever before continued the expansion of collectivism ideology. If Great Depression turned the direction of America ideology, World War II added fuel to that journey.

Under a mixed ideology, FDR proposed Economic Bill of Rights in 1944 to guarantee an individual: Employment with a living wage; Freedom from unfair competition and monopolies; Housing, Medical care, Education, and, Social security.

The claim of right to housing, medical care, education and pension, is fundamentally false. If consuming is a right, where are those materials and services coming from? From heaven? If an individual produces food or builds house, the person should have the right to the result. Anyone claim right to the result can only be by force or looting. Government has no way to guarantee job, food, and income to anybody, without resorting to force or abusing of power. All material productions are made by individuals and belong to those productive individuals.

Employment can happen only when the demand of labor and supply of labor reaches the equilibrium. There is no such thing as guaranteed employment in a free economy. A hiring can happen when the person has the skill to accomplish certain function of work. Government's intervention of labor market, either by hiring unnecessarily in government agencies, or by manipulating tax codes or monetary policy, creates inefficiency, corruption, favoritism, inflation, and waste of resources

So are the cases with housing, medical care and education. Housing, medical care and education are created or serviced by people, and can only be gained with trade (money for service) between those providing the service and those creating service. Government's guarantee only means one thing on the market place: a forced transfer.

Hence, economic Bill of Rights can happen only when the government uses the legal force to transfer income (in the form of various taxations) from certain members of the society to the others. When government guarantee right to some, it deprives right from the other. Injustice replaces justice in America. And transfer of individual rights should not be in the power of US government!

Chapter 5 - Restore Gold Standard and Dollar's Value

Aug 15, 1971, Sunday, President Nixon appeared on prime TV and made a 15 min speech about his new economic policy. Battered by high inflation, war spending, slow economic growth, and ever-higher trade deficit and budget deficit, Nixon made an inevitable choice to delink dollar and gold. This was a historical turning point, because dollar, the official legal tender of USA since 1776, has been always defined by its equivalence to certain amount of gold, and freely convertible to gold at US Treasury. Although this conversion was suspended from time to time, such as during war times, Great Depression, and since 1968 to US citizen, dollar was always defined by its value to gold. Upon this gold standard, America rose from small colonies in wild jungles to world's most successful, most powerful nation.

"...We must protect the position of the American dollar as a pillar of monetary stability around the world. In the past 7 years, there has been an average of one international monetary crisis every year. Now who gains from these crises? Not the workingman; not the investor; not the real producers of wealth. The gainers are the international money speculators. Because they thrive on crises, they help to create them.

In recent weeks, the speculators have been waging an all-out war on the American dollar. The strength of a nation's currency is based on the strength of that nation's economy--and the American economy is by far the strongest in the world. Accordingly, I have directed the Secretary of the Treasury to take the action necessary to defend the dollar against the speculators.

I have directed Secretary Connally to suspend temporarily the convertibility of the dollar into gold or other reserve assets, except in amounts and conditions determined to be in the interest of monetary stability and in the best interests of the United States."

Nixon was one of the most shrewd politicians in history, as in this speech, he lied in many aspects: the "temporary" suspension has not returned for over forty years; he blamed the "speculator" for the weakness of dollar when real culprit was the fault of politicians on building "Great Society" and fighting Vietnam War. The irresponsible, persistent big spending by politicians flooded the global market with cheap, paper dollar. Whoever held those paper bills would convert to gold without any hesitations.

Dollar Was Backed by Gold Standard Since Beginning

The Dollar was pegged to gold since the establishment of the United States as the founding fathers were strongly against a fiat currency. Indeed, they made it un-constitutional for government to issue paper currency. After gaining independence, the newly established Republic strongly adhered to Adam Smith's classic economic theory and adopted a strict gold standard. The Dollar was defined by the Constitution in 1789, at a value of $18.65 per ounce. (1 dollar contained 1.604 gram of gold). Alexander Hamilton designed a bimetal system, which allowed both gold and silver to the legal tender at a fixed ration of 1:15. Silver coins were used by most people in daily transaction, while gold coins in big deals.

The peg of dollar and gold was briefly suspended during Civil War, but resumed convertibility in 1879, at a face value of $20.67 per ounce. By then, major European countries also adopted gold standard. America maintained gold standard till 1933, when President Roosevelt ordered all US citizens to deliver their gold holdings to Federal Reserve Bank, and illegalized private ownership of gold coins, bars and certificates.

In 1944, central bankers from G7 countries, gathered at New Hampshire's Bretton Woods resort, and reached an agreement that linked world currencies to Dollar, and US Federal Reserve bank promised to redeem dollars to gold at request. Ever since, most international trades were settled in dollar, and most central bank kept their foreign reserves in dollar. A new pyramid of world currency order, based on gold-dollar-other currencies, was in place. The Dollar became the only reserve currency of the world.

That reserve currency status was double-edged. The post-war Bretton Woods system establish the dollar as the only reserve currency of the world, upon which other major currency were pegged, and only dollar was pegged to gold. The reserve status instantly created huge demand for the dollar by other central banks as "reserve", and commercial banks for international trades and investments. Politicians use the dollar status to finance ever-increasing budget deficits and trade deficits. Those deficits did not weaken the dollar initially, because the international demand for dollar. Nevertheless, as more and more paper dollar were created, its intrinsic value drop below its gold peg. Those countries with trade surplus, such as UK and France, would inevitably convert their dollar to gold.

The Fed's gold reserve reached an all time high in 1949 at 21,828 tons, representing 71% of global monetary gold bullion reserve of 30,623 tons. Under the Bretton Woods, other central banks had the right to redeem their dollar to gold at $35 per ounce any time they wanted.

In 1960, gold reserve of the Fed reduced to 15,822 tons, as foreign central banks redeem their dollar for gold at the Fed. Through the 1960s, Fed was losing gold at a rapid pace, by 1970, Fed was left with only 9,839 tons.

In Jan 1970, Nixon picked Arthur Burns as the new Fed Chairman who opened the print press of the Fed, to finance the war and Nixon's pet social programs. Federal fund rate was reduced from 9% in June 1969 to 3% in Feb 1971. Under low rate and loose monetary policy, gold was flying out of Fed's vault. When Nixon abandoned gold standard in Aug 1971, the Fed was left with only 8,133 tons gold, which has not changed ever since.

Gold reserve by Fed Reserve bank (tons)

25,000
20,000
15,000
10,000
5,000
0

1948 1954 1960 1966 1972 1978 1984 1990 1996 2002 2008

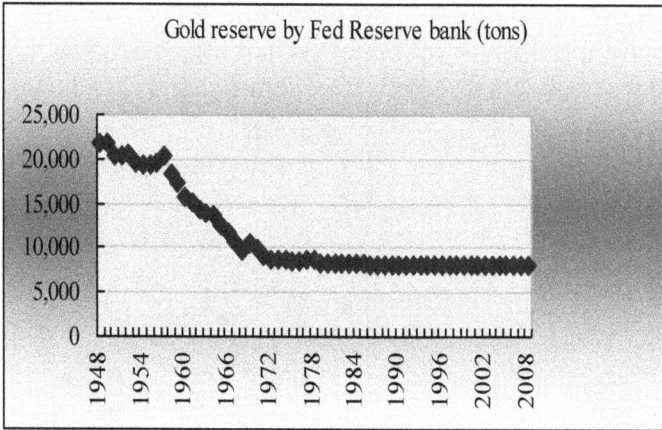

Source: Federal Reserve Bank

Gold has played a more important role as a monetary tool than as a beautiful, decorative metal. Although derided as a barbarian currency, gold's potential role and function as a monetary tool regained status after the financial crisis.

Very few have realized the link between the gold standard and the political system. Gold standard in the monetary system means a true democratic social system, in which the government interferes minimally with the business and finance of the society. Under gold standard, government cannot create money, unless backed with new acquired gold reserves. Business and finance can fully function without the presence of the government. When gold was the world currency during the 19th century, globalization and free trade reached a pinnacle that cannot be matched.

Once gold was removed from monetary system, the government took full control of money issuing, interest rate, and inflation. They can print as much money as they wish, if inflation is not out of control and there is no revolt on the street. They invented central banking, which serves as the printing press of the government. Gold is the obstacle for government to control the supply of money and the cost of money. Therefore, abandoning gold standard was bankers and politician common goal, and they achieved it worldwide.

Should the world return to gold standard? What are the pros and cons of selecting gold as the once and forever money for human society?

3000 Years of History, One Constant Gold Value

Gold is the best measurement and storage of value, after trying many different forms of money in human history. Land has intrinsic value, and always goes up in monetary terms. However land right can be confiscated or lost. A house can store value, but building materials decay over time and the property cannot be carried away. Stocks and bonds can generate handsome returns, but they can also lose a person's fortune.

Gold standard limits the amount of money a central bank can issue and money stock in circulation. Roy Jastram demonstrated that Britain went through inflation and deflation periods during 200 years of gold standard, but "gold maintains its purchasing power over long periods of time, for example, half century intervals" (source: Roy Jastram, *The Golden Constant*, p132).

Here is the annual income of several professions in the ancient Roman Empire. The stipends were quoted in Denari, a common silver coin that was 1/25 of Aureus, which was the most common gold coin at the time. Aureus was coined at 1/40 Roman pound (8 gram) during Julius Caesar's time, but was reduced to 1/50 Roman pound (6.5 gram) during the Aurelius reign. (This was the same trick to create inflation in entire history).

A Senator would earn 86 ounce of gold per year, and equestrian Knight would earn 17 ounce of gold during the same period. I assume that the stipend for a Legionary Soldier was about the average income for the citizens, 33 ounce a year. 33 ounce of gold today is worth about $39,235 in 2009. If female family members did not earn any income, the listed income would be equivalent to today's household income. In today's term,

$39,235 annual household income is very similar to the average income in developed countries.

Job	Denari / month	Annual stipend (in Denari)	in gold ounce	in 2010 dollar
Secretary	15	180	1.6	1,962
Lecturer	12	144	1.3	1,569
Messenger	9	108	1.0	1,177
Haruspex (fortune teller)	10	120	1.1	1,308
Legionary Soldier (Private)	20	240	2.2	2,616
Praetorian (guard in Rome)	60	720	6.5	7,847
Knights (equestrian order)	NA	NA	17	20,692
Legionary Soldier (Centurion)	300	3,600	33	39,235
Senators	NA	NA	86	103,458

Source: Institute of Governmental Affairs, University of California, Davis, and ancientcoins.biz

If we compare Roman's income level with US per capita income in recent history, they are in a very close range. Since 1935, the average US per capita income were in a range of 20-100 ounce. When the US economy was in recession periods or was experiencing high inflation, income in gold term fell. When the economy was strong, income rose. Productivity gain should have contributed to the rise of income; however, productivity should not affect the measurement of income in gold. As humans gained efficiency in producing goods and services, we also gained efficiency in finding and producing gold, although not necessarily in a linear relationship.

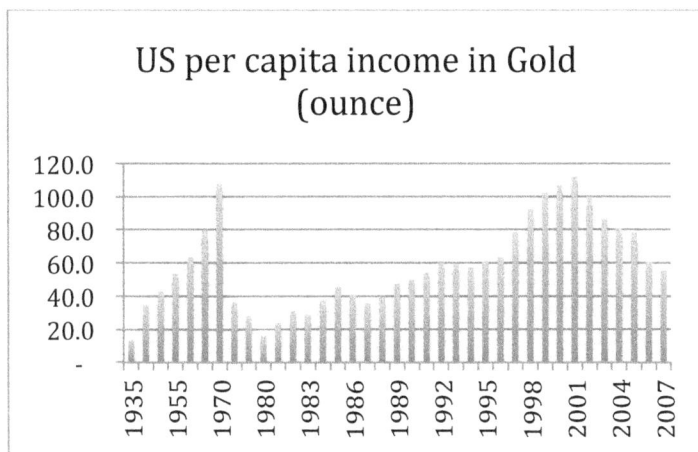

US per capita income in Gold (ounce)

Source: U.S. Department of Commerce, Bureau of Economic Analysis, www.bea.gov/doc

Comparing with median incomes in developed countries, we can also see that they were in a range of 50-80 ounce of gold in recent years.

Country	Median income (national	Year	PPP rate (OEC	Median househol d income	Incom e in Gold

	currency)		D)	(PPP)	ounce
Switzerland	109,236 CHF	2008	1.68	$64,877	79
Canada	63,900 CAD	2008	1.23	$51,951	63
United States	49,777 USD	2009	1.00	$49,777	61
Australia	66,890 AUD	2007	1.52	$44,115	54
New Zealand	63,867 NZD	2008	1.59	$40,214	49
United Kingdom	24,700 GBP	2004	0.63	$39,000	88
Israel	107,820 ILS	2006	2.90	$37,000	83
Ireland	35,410 EUR	2005	1.02	$35,000	79
United Kingdom	21,892 GBP	2005	0.65	$34,000	76
Hong Kong	186,000 HKD	2005	5.96	$31,000	70
Singapore	45,960 SGD	2005	1.55	$30,000	67

Source: US Census Bureau, Department of Commerce, Federal Reserve Bank

Based on the book *History of Compensation System in Ancient China*,中国俸禄制度史, I found the annual salary data of governmental officials in 2000 years of history. To make the comparison easy, I chose the salary for County official, the 7th rank of governmental officials as the benchmark. Through history, the salaries for officials were quoted in quantity of rice, in silk fabrics, in copper coins, and in silver. Converting those values into gold was based on the book and other historical records. This income level is certainly above the average income at the time, and should be close to the upper middle class' income level.

Currently, a similar position in China should have an income of 100,000-200,000, translating into 10-20 ounce of gold based on today's gold price, which is similar to China's average urban income. This data supports that average income level, as measured by the amount of gold, has been very stable and consistent through the history of civilization. Median incomes, ranging from ancient Roman and ancient China, to USA, HK and Israel contemporarily, fell between 10-90 ounces of gold.

County Official Salary	Time period, AD	Salary in gold, ounce
Southern/Northern	420–589	24
Sui	581–618	96
Tang	618–907	96
Jin	1115–1234	26
Yuan	1271–1368	72
Ming	1368–1644	9
Qing	1644-1911	33
Current county head	1949-	10-20
Source: History of Compensation System in Ancient China,中国俸禄制度史		

Through the history of civilization and across the world, gold provides a measurement of value for an individual's wealth and income. Owning gold is a good way to preserve wealth. Due to risks of all types, preserving wealth over time and space is a challenge. Paper money does not hold value over the long run. Land cannot be carried or deposited. Business can fail. Only gold can be stored and transported, and can maintain its value over time.

Additional study conducted by Goldman Sachs economic research team (based on USGS and GFMS databases) showed that rom 1900 to 2000, real gold price per ounce, measured in 2008 US Dollar, is unbelievably constant! There were many ups and downs in the price through the century, but the long-term average has been around $400/ounce for over a hundred years. All those data strongly supports that gold is the best measurement of value in entire human history.

Karl Marx once said, "Although gold and silver are not by nature money, money is by nature gold and silver."

Does the world have enough gold as currency? Of the 161,000 tons of above ground gold ever mined in history, about 30,000 tons are held by central banks. US Fed holds 8,134 tons, followed by Germany, IMF, France, and Italy. About 55% of the gold stock was mined after 1955.

The world's total of official gold reserves was estimated to be 700 tons in 1870 and The Bank of England, as the central bank of the system, had reserves of 161 tons in 1870. In 1913, prior to World War I, total reserves increased to 8,100 tons. The United States had 2,293 tons, Russia 1,233 tons, France 1,030 tons, Argentina 440 tons, Germany 439 tons, Austria 378 tons and Italy 356 tons.

The table below shows the amount of gold held by major central banks as of 2008. Total reserve held by central banks was stable since World War II, ranging from 29,700 to 38,000 tons. US reserve peaked in 1950s at 21,828 and reduced to about 9,000 tons in 1971, in which year the dollar was de-pegged from gold. Today, US gold reserve is 8,134 tons.

Gold reserve by major central banks (tons, as of 2008)

United States	8,133
Germany	3,413
France	2,492
Italy	2,452
Switzerland	1,040
IMF	3,217
Central banks total	29,785

Source: WGC

Entire gold stock that was ever mined on earth is estimated to be about 160K tons. Because gold cannot be destroyed and is chemically stable, gold only changes hands and changes forms. Half of gold stocks exist as jewelry, with the rest as bullions and fabrications.

Usage pattern of world gold stock (tons, 2008 data)	
Jewelry	82,700
Central banks	29,784
ETFs/Bullions	26,500
Fabrication	19,200
Other	3,600
Total	161,784

Source: WGC

Did Oil Cause Inflation?

The rise of oil price was blamed for causing most of inflation in the 70s. Oil shock triggered global panic buying in 1973 and 1979, bringing oil price to a record high. Dollar inflation was covered in this ever-rising oil price, which was caused by short-term imbalance of demand and supply.

Let's check the number carefully. In 1970, oil was trading at $2.9/barrel, or **1/12** ounce of gold, when $35 was equal to 1 ounce of gold.

In 1973 before the oil shock, when dollar was depreciated to $100/ounce, oil was still $2.9/barrel, or 1/35 ounce of gold.

In 1974, oil price was raised to $10/barrel, and dollar was $120/ounce, oil was again around **1/12** ounce of gold.

In last 40 years, despite all the volatility, oil price has not changed much from its 1/12 ounce of gold.

What the OPEC did was simply raise the oil price to keep it in line with inflation. Oil did not cause inflation. To the contrary, inflation caused the oil price to rise in dollar terms. Oil price in ounce of gold has been constant in last four decades.

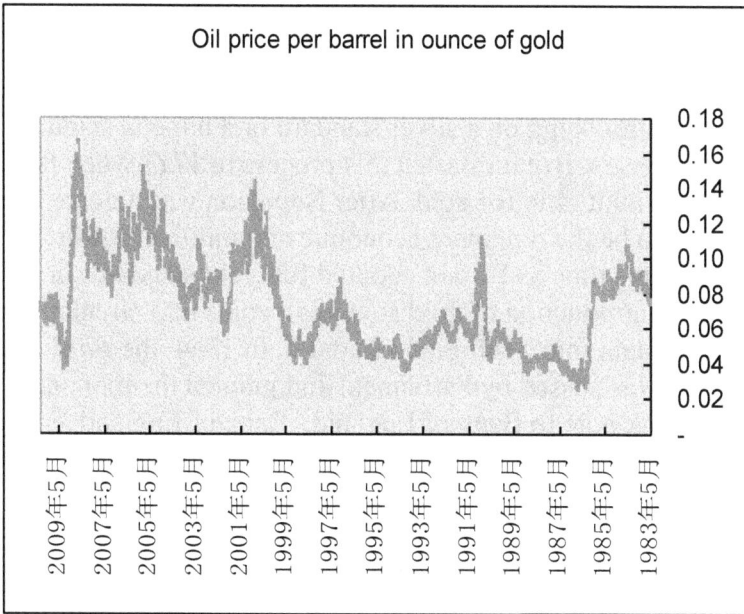

Oil price per barrel in ounce of gold

Source: Bloomberg

Gold standard = Democracy, Fiat currency = Authoritarianism

The major economies of the world adopted gold standard in the 19th century after being on a silver standard or a bimetal standard for near 400 years. Britain started this process in 1717 when Isaac Newton set a mint ratio for gold. After Napoleon was defeated, Britain rose to be the dominant economic and military power, at almost the same time as Britain adopted full gold standard. In 1817, the re-introduction of gold sovereign coins into circulation converted Britain into a full gold standard. In 1844, the *Bank Charter Act* was passed by Parliament and granted the monopoly of issuing bank note to Bank of England. Bank of England backed all its notes with gold reserves.

Under the influence of Bank of England, most major economies also adopted gold standard, with Canada in 1853, Australia in 1865, and Germany in 1873. United States was on a bimetal standard since 1792. After passing 1900 *Gold Standard Act*, dollar was defined at $20.67 per ounce, and America adopted a full gold standard.

Gold became the worldwide currency. The gold standard facilitated global trade and economic growth. In 19th century, Britain and America achieved tremendous economic expansion that was never experienced before. During the century, Industrial Revolution spread to most parts of the world, productivity gained astonishingly with buildup of railway systems, with ocean trade running on steamships, with invention of electricity, and with factories driven by engines. Globalization reached a level that would not be matched until 100 years later.

Under the gold standard, central bank was the sole (private) institution that was authorized to issue bank notes. Central banks backed issuing of currency with their gold reserves and honored to redeem the currency notes into gold. Hence, money supply was determined by gold stock in each country.

From 1820s to 1913, the world currencies, called Dollar, Pound, Franc, were pegged to gold. This pegging system was disrupted during war times, such as America Civil War, but America resumed to the gold standard post the war. World War I disrupted this system again, when Britain announced stopped redeem pound to gold and rest of European countries followed.

After World War I, Britain was determined to resume the gold standard at the pre-war level. To restore the value of sterling and to re-establish sterling as the world reserve currency, Bank of England and Federal Reserve Bank worked together to restore the pound's value. At that time, Britain had passed its peak of economic and military power. It needed America's help. It could not single-handedly return Sterling to be the world reserve currency.

In 1925, dollar and sterling based gold exchange standard was established. All currencies were exchangeable to sterling and dollar, and only sterling and dollar could be exchanged to gold at 2 central banks. A new world currency order was established with the Dollar being a world leader on the stage.

In 1949, the Fed had gold reserve of 21,828 tons, and money in circulation (M0) was $27.5 billion. By then, the dollar was pegged to gold at $35/ounce. With 21,828 tons of gold, the Fed could issue $24.6 billion of dollars. Gold backing was **90%** that year.

	Money in circulatio n	Gold reserve (tons)	Money backed by Gold reserve at spot price ($billion)

	($billion)		
1949	27.5	21,828	24.6
2009	915	8,133	261

Source: Federal Reserve Bank

Fast-forward 50 years, in 2009, the Fed's gold reserve stood at 8,133 tons, and money in circulation was $915 billion. Gold price was $970 at year-end 2009. Theoretically, Fed could issue only $261 billion of dollar with 8,133 tons of gold: Gold backing dropped to **29%.** If the Fed promises to redeem every dollar in circulation to gold, the dollar has to be depreciated by 70%, to a level of $3500/ounce. Unfortunately, the dollar has long been de-linked from gold - Fed does not have to redeem a single dollar to gold.

President Reagan seriously intended to return dollar to gold during his campaign. He even recorded a commercial in 1980 before his New Hampshire primary, promising a return to gold standard as his campaign promise. Unfortunately, that ad never broadcast publicly. Reagan was talked out of the plan by his monetary advisors. Nevertheless, he supported the Gold Commission to seriously review the pros and cons of restoring dollar to gold standard.

The Commission was to "conduct a study to assess and make recommendations with regard to the policy of the U.S. Government concerning the role of gold in domestic and international monetary systems"

The final report by the Commission failed to recommend restoring gold standard in US, and to force Fed fixing monetary based and gold reserve. This commission is pre-destined to reach such conclusion, because representation and selection of its committee member. Abandoning gold standard had massively benefited bankers who profit from unlimited paper money issuing and inflation. Those bankers have formed the most powerful interest group in Washington, and brainwashed so-called elite economists, hired at Fed, Treasury, IMF, university, Wall Street. Any commission convened from this circle, explicitly and implicitly, serve the interest of bankers. Even the President could hardly swing its conclusion.

During a helicopter flight to Andrews air force base in 1981, President Reagan told Ron Paul that "no great nation that abandoned the gold standard has remained a great country" (Source: *End The Fed*, Ron Paul, 2009) Mr. Ron Paul has been a Congress man from Texas for 14 terms, who has adamantly fought for restoration of gold standard in America.

Despite giving up the gold standard, Fed under the leadership of Chairman Volcker and Greenspan, generally followed the principle to achieve stable price policy. Not only did Volcker brought inflation under control, but also a relatively tight policy was in place during his term. American economy experienced the longest post war period of economic expansion during the Volcker-Greenspan years. The conservative monetary policy clearly reflected by stable gold price and low inflation during this period.

Most intriguing figure is Alan Greenspan, who wrote "Gold and Economic Freedom" and published in 1966 *The Objectivity* newsletter, circulated by libertarian philosopher Ayn Rand. In his biography, he called the article "probably most incendiary essay", criticized government for its natural tendency to spend beyond means, "deficit spending is simply a scheme for the confiscation of wealth. Gold stands in the way of this insidious process."

With the absolute power to control money supply, the Fed cannot resist the temptation to print money, whenever it deemed necessary. Politicians' unchecked fiscal spending on the Vietnam War in 1960s and on welfare programs, added more pressure for the Fed to keep the rate low. Treasure and Fed collaborated on issuing more debt, and printing more money. Not doubt that, those money printings and deficit caused high inflationary in 70s, weak dollar and eventual redeeming of gold by trading partners.

"Legally increasing the money supply is just as immoral as the counterfeiter who illegally prints money. The new paper money has value only because it steals its "value" from the existing stock of paper money." *The Case For Gold*, Ron Paul P173)

Historically, the Roman Empire used similar strategies to print money to pay for astonishing spending. When the Roman Empire was on its rise, its currency, with heavy gold or silver contents, was strong and widely accepted. When Roman emperors spent more than taxation revenue, debase its currency was the path they took.

Because tax collection was difficult and raising tax rates was dangerous, the easiest way to finance spending was to mint coins with less gold content. Initially those slightly counterfeited currencies were not noticed, and were accepted by its citizens and created temporary prosperity on the surface. Over time, people realized that there were too many (bad) coins on the market place, while the amount of goods and services available was the same as before, price level started to rise, and inflation happened. During late years of Roman Empire, inflation went out of control, citizen lost confidence in money, and slaves rebelled.

Similar situations happened again and again. War finance was the most common reason for government to use its minting machine. War spending had to be financed, and the easiest way of financing was issuing debt through the central bank. Eventually, the newly issued debt (and money), without backing of gold or value, diluted the value of existing money stocks. Each unit of money would have less purchase power, i.e. inflation occurred.

"Money that obtains its status from government decree alone is arbitrary, indefinable, and is destined to fail, for it will eventually be rejected by the people. Since today's paper money achieves its status by government declaration and not by its value in itself, eventually total power over the economy must be granted to the monopolists who manage the monetary system." (*The Case For Gold*, Ron Paul P187)

China experienced hype inflation in Yuan dynasty before the empire collapsed, and again in Ming dynasty before Qing took over, and again in 1940s under during Civil War. In recent years, America financed its two Iraq wars by issuing debt to foreign investors, and created significant depreciation of dollar.

History repeats itself.

Why is Deflation Bad for the Economy?

After abandoning gold standard for 40 years, economists today "unanimously" agree that restoring gold is "absolutely impossible". Restoring gold standard seems so ridiculous and barbarian. Why is the gold standard "impossible" and "barbarian" ? What is different today from 1971?

One common argument against gold standard is: gold standard will cause deflation, which is really bad and can cause global recession and economic collapse. Central banks use its policy tools to prevent deflation from happening and also to keep inflation in control. The famous speech, given by "helicopter" Bernanke in Nov 2002, "Deflation: making sure "it" doesn't happen here", well illustrated Fed's believing.

Deflation is bad because "falling price levels tend to lead to labor unrest, strikes, unemployment and radical movements generally" (*Economics*, 8th edition, Paul Samuelson, p629). The leading Keynesian economist, Paul Samuelson, was sharply critical of gold standard. Samuelson said that the gold standard was historically deflationary, because "The long term supply of gold cannot possibly keep up with the liquidity needs of growing international trade"(*Economics*, 8th edition, p697).

Nevertheless, in history book, social turmoil and unrest were never preceded by periods of deflation, but always period of **inflation**, particularly hype inflation, that brought down empires, kingdoms, and dynasties. When inflation was rampant, the society was destined for rebellions, unrests and even revolutions. For example:

- Prior to the French Revolution, government was near bankruptcy due to heavy borrowing to finance numerous wars. Price level was up 1,153% in 1796.

- After World War I, to repay war reparation, Weimar Republic engaged unprecedented borrowing that created hype inflation of 730,000,000,000 % in 1923.

- The breakup of Yugoslavia was accompanied by inflation of 331,000,000% in 1994.

- V. I. Lenin once said "The way to crush bourgeoisie is to grind them between the millstones of taxation and inflation". In Russia 1923, inflation reached 60,806,000% (source: Bank of England)

Inflation erodes the value of savings that people worked very hard to accumulate, and benefits those who have borrowed money and spent. It distorts the value system of a society, hence, it creates social tension and unfairness. Because inflation discourages saving and encourages spending, the society become speculative, short sighted and unstable. Inflation is a robbery of people's hard-earned wealth.

Doesn't deflation encourage people to save and to invest wisely? Who, as a citizen, would object to having money that has increasing purchase power? Slight deflation would be beneficial to a society that encourages people to save, to build a sound social value system and a stable society.

For example, in Britain from 1698 to 1914, the Pound was pegged to gold and stayed in a close range for over 200 years. During that period, Britain underwent Industrial Revolution and the fastest economic expansion. Britain became the economic, military and political dominant power in the world. The stable pound was rightfully accredited to Britain's stable society, family values and global dominance.

Similar view was shared by Michael D. Bordo, that "wholesale price index was relatively stable under the classic gold standard in Great Britain (1821-1914), and the US (1834-1861 and 1879-1933) than afterwards when both countries adopted a far greater discretionary fiat money standard, see figures below. In both countries, the trend line was slightly deflationary under the classic gold standard. (Source: Michael. D. Bordo, *The Gold Standard: Myths and Realities*, p211-214)

Can an economy grow healthily in an environment of slightly deflation? Look at the historical economy data of Britain. From 1800 to 1914, while the wholesale price level declined ~25%, GDP in 1914 was 2.3 times of 1800!

Wholesale price index in UK, 1800-1979

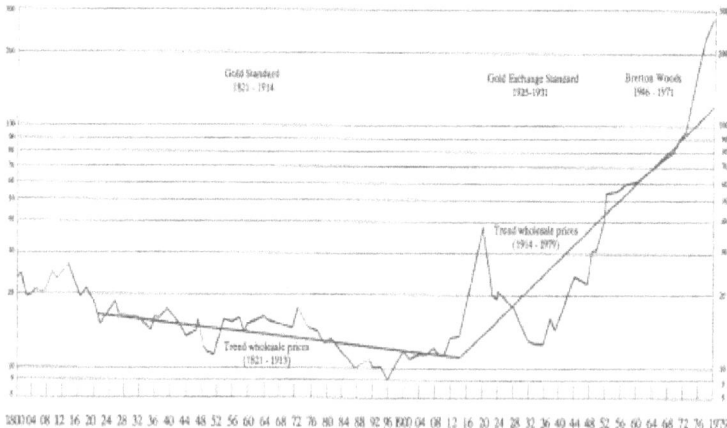

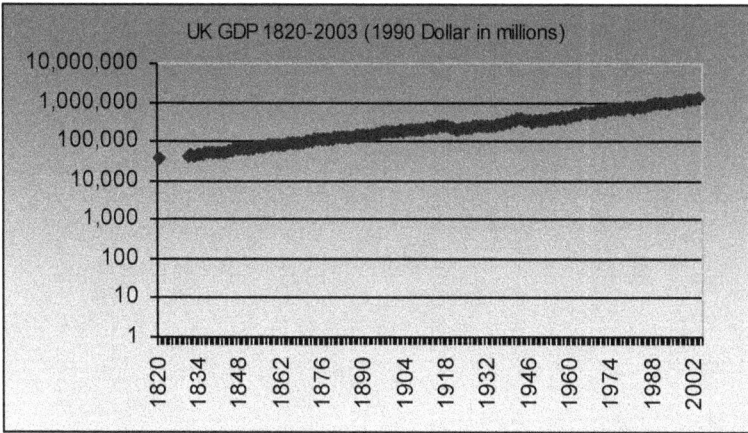

Source: Angus Maddison, GGDC. Michael. D. Bordo, *The Gold Standard: Myths and Realities*

In US, from 1800 to 1914, wholesale price level declined ~32%. At the same time, GDP in 1914 was 4.9 times of 1800!

Wholesale Price Index, USA, 1880-1979

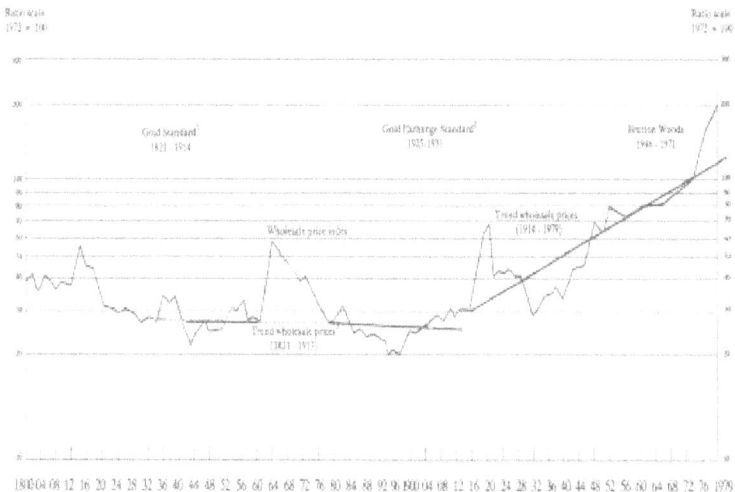

US GDP 1820-2003, (1990 Dollar, in million),

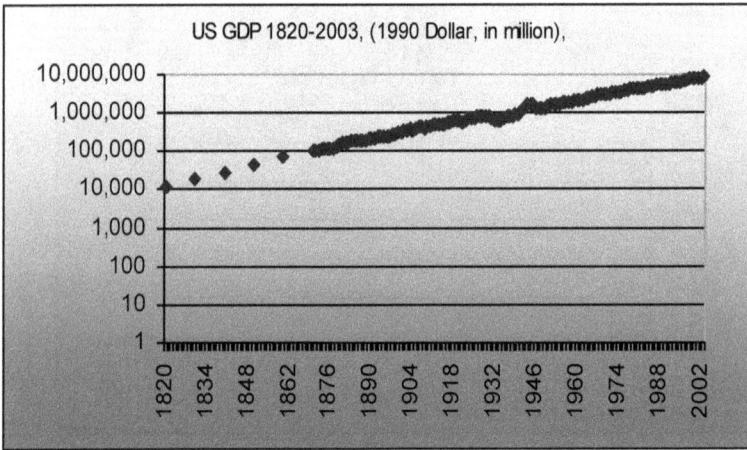

Source: Michael. D. Bordo, *The Gold Standard: Myths and Realitie*s. and Angus Maddison, GGDC.

"It is difficult to believe that prices actually fell throughout most of the 19th century and well into the 20th. Aside from wartime and a few other unusual episodes in the 19th century, machines manufactured goods more cheaply, and as transportation of goods improved, prices declined because the value of the currency was fixed to gold and silver."

"In the 25 years following the Civil War in the US, wholesale prices declined by an average of 60%. And in some areas, such as textiles, the decline proved even steeper and more substantial. Most goods in 1900 were cheaper than they had been in 1800. In only a little over 25 yeas, between 1872 and 1897, one dollar could buy 43% more rice than in 1872, 35% more beans, 49% more tea, 51% more roasted coffee, 114% more sugar, 62% more mutton, 25% more fresh port, 60% more lard and butter, and 42% more milk. " (Source: Jack Weatherford: *The History of Money*. p205)

Hence, the greatest economic growth and success in Britain and America was built upon gold standard and deflation. Founding fathers were strongly against fiat currency. When their currencies were strong and stable, trading partner like to deal with them and society were stable and productive. Since Great Depression, this inflation trick permeated among policy makers, and polluted whole society.

Politicians were short sighted because they had to be elected to have a job. Under pressure of elections, inflation boom became their favorite dish on the menu because it was instant, visible, and euphoric. They lost vision and responsibility for the country. Loving power and influence is in the blood of politicians. They love to levy more tax so that they can spend more, and have more influence. Handing out money (tax exemptions, subsidies, welfares, government procurement etc.) to this special group and that special group made politicians popular. To do that, they needed money. And they found out that the most magical way of getting money is by printing more!

This evidence shows us that the world does not need inflation to have a healthy economy. Inflation is a hidden tax that no one ever voted against. Inflation is a robbery of people!

"We are now so conditioned by permanent price inflation that the idea of prices *falling* every year is difficult to grasp. And yet, prices generally fell every year from the beginning of the Industrial Revolution in the latter part of the eighteenth century until 1940, with the exception of periods of major war, when the governments inflated the money supply radically and drove up prices, after which they would gradually fall once more. We have to realize that falling prices did not mean depression, since costs were falling due to increased productivity, so that profits were not sinking. (Source: *The Case Against The Fed,* Murray Rothbard*)*

Unfortunately, Rothbard was in a minority camp, and mainstream economists today believe that inflation is "necessary" for the economic growth.

Inflation targeting has replaced money supply targeting, becoming the mainstream practice to set monetary policy since 1980s of global central banks. The justification for targeted inflation is that deflation is disastrous for economy. We need inflation so that GDP growth can be stimulated; and unemployment will be kept low. To prevent deflation from happening, central banks need inflation as a buffer, usually a mild 1-3% per year.

The need for inflation is well articulated and advocated by generations of Keynesian economists. They told us that inflation is good and necessary for an economy to function because the depreciation of money drives people to consume. Without inflation, savings would be too high, and economic growth would stagnate.

Their arguments sound very convincing. Before accepting their thoughts, let us listen to another great thinker: "The trouble with paper money is that it rewards the minority that can manipulate money and makes fools of the generation that has worked and saved. "(Source: Adam Smith)

And from Keynes himself: "By a continuous process of inflation, governments can confiscate, secretly and unobserved, an important part of the wealth of their citizens. By this method, they not only confiscate, but they confiscate arbitrarily; and while the process impoverishes many, it actually enriches some" (Source: John Maynard Keynes , *The Economic Consequences of Peace*)

"Inflation is theft and literally steals wealth from one group for the benefit of another." (Source: *The Case For Gold*, Ron Paul)

To justify the existence of central banks, politicians have to prove that monetary policy adds value to managing the economy. It is difficulty to prove that central bankers can time the business cycle well enough to set right monetary policies that maximize GDP growth, keep unemployment low, and reduce business cycle. In the long run, can the wisdom of central bankers do a better job managing the money supply than a fixed supply of gold? or a fixed supply of fiat currency, as once suggested by Friedman?

There is no way to construct two identical economies, with one on gold standard, and another on fiat currency, to prove that one is a better monetary system than the other. There are a myriad of factors that affect economic growth and business volatility in any given time. It is impossible to design and conduct economic experiments as in natural sciences, where empirical evidence is the king.

Similarly, a time series of GDP growth rate in one society before and after adopting gold standard will not be conclusive. The reason is that GDP growth is heavily affected by population growth, technological revolution, global expansion, and medical advancement. It is impossible to keep those factors constant over a meaningful period of time and test the impact of gold standard. In the end, there is no evidence to prove that GDP growth is stronger, unemployment is lower, price level is more stable, under a fiat money system than under the gold standard.

In 1981, a research paper by Federal Reserve Bank of St. Louis stated that, "economic performance in US and UK was superior under classic gold standard to that of subsequent period of managed fiduciary money."

The most famous conclusion about gold standard was made by Friedman and Schwartz, "the blind, un-designed, and quasi-automatic working of the gold standard turned out to produce a greater measure of predictability and regularity-perhaps because its discipline was impersonal and inescapable-than did deliberate and conscious control exercised within institutional arrangements intended to promote stability" (Source: Friedman and Schwartz, *A Monetary History of the United States, p 10)*

Impact of Gold Standard on GDP Growth

The fact that central banks can increase and decrease money supply is a double-edged sword. Inflation booms can be created by printing money, hence politicians love inflation. If US had adopted an inflationary fiat currency, would the real GDP have grown faster?

Annual gold production grew at CAGR of 1.6%, from 386 tons in 1900 to 2,300 tons in 2008. Worldwide real GDP growth was 3.0% during the same period. (Source: Angus Maddison GGDC) If the world economies had been gold specie standard, price level should have deflated 1.4% per year. Because the world was not in gold standard through the period, inflation has occurred and fluctuated meaningfully from period to period, and from country to country.

Let's look at some historical US economic data.

US	GDP growth		Inflation	
1867 - 1914	3.7%		0.1%	Gold standard
1929- 1970	3.2%		1.5%	Gold standard
1970- 2009	2.9%		4.4%	Greenback standard

Source: Federal Reserve Bank, St Louis and Angus Maddison GGDC.

There is no doubt that inflation was lower under gold standard than under fiat currency. In US, from 1867 to 1914 under classic gold standard, inflation was 0.1% per year, and from 1929 to 1970 under gold exchange standard, inflation was 1.5% per year. After abandoning gold standard, from 1970 to 2009, inflation averaged 4.4% in US.

Under gold standard, from 1867 to 1914, US grew its GDP grew at CAGR of 3.7%; and from 1929 to 1970 at 3.2% per year. GDP grew at 2.9% from 1970-2009 after abandoning gold standard in 1971. **GDP growth was faster in US under gold standard than that under greenback standard.**

What is the mission of the Fed again?

Does GDP grow faster under gold standard than under fiat currency? It is a question almost impossible to answer because GDP growth is affected by too many factors, and US economic structure has changed during the period. It was the fastest growing economy from 1867-1960s. Its economy slowed down after the immigration process slowed and industrialization completed. Measuring the impact of monetary policy alone on GDP growth is an impossible task. In the long run, GDP growth is mostly affected with population growth. There were periods in history that GDP grew faster than population growth, such as during Industrial Revolution and technology revolution; and there were periods that GDP grew slower than population, such as major wartime and Black Death.

Should the world use gold as currency again, global economy would be in a slightly tight monetary condition. Assuming the world economy can grow at 3% in the long run, it will be constrained by gold production growth of 1.6% per year. Gold standard means that the world will have an appreciating currency and the cost of capital will be slightly higher. But there is nothing wrong to have a constantly tight monetary supply and an appreciating currency. The market condition will encourage people to save, to avoid asset bubble, and to avoid speculative investments.

There are many ways to solve the need for liquidity under gold standard, particularly in a digital age, nearly all transactions are done by computers' debit and credit. There is nearly no need for real coins. But taking the power of printing money away from bankers and politicians, gold standard give people what they deserve: wealth created by their hands. No stealing, no deficit spending, and no asset bubble!

At least, a gold exchange standard can be restored, similar to Bretton Woods system, money supply can be managed by adjusting reserve ratio under fractional reserve system. Although some argue that there is no real difference between a banking system of fractional reserve of fiat money and of fractional reserve of gold, gold reserve system adds confidence to the currency, and limits supplying of money. If government spends like drunken sailor, which Nixon did, gold will fly out of central bank and threaten survival of the government.

Chapter 6 - Dismantle The Federal Reserve Bank

Widespread banking crisis hit world financial markets every decade or so. Economic disaster of Great Depression is well known and documented. Since World War II, the crisis hit Sweden in the 60s, United Kingdom in the 70s, United States in the 80s with saving and loan banks, Brazil, Thailand and Turkey in the 90s, and of course, the crisis of all crisis in 2008.

Great Depression started with collapse at Wall Street, when Dow Jones dropped 47%, from 381 in Sep 1929, to 200 in Nov 1929. And market continued its free fall to the low of 42 in July 1932, a shocking loss of 89% from the peak of the market. The financial crash caused bankruptcy of nine thousands banks, loss of saving by millions families, unemployment rate at 21%, drop of crop prices 60%. The crisis spread to the world market, caused the most severe global economic recession in history.

From the peak in January '73 to the low in December '74, the Dow Jones Industrial lost 46%, while the S&P 500 lost 36% during the same period. Consequently, unemployment hit 9% in 1975, the highest since Great Depression. Inflation hit double digits and did not tame down until Volcker took over the Fed in 1980 and raised discount rate numerous times. Following "go-go 60s" when economic growth was "unparalleled, unprecedented, and uninterrupted" Politicians took very measure to tax, to borrow and to spend, on Vietnam War, on Cold War, on Great Society, on moon landing and on welfares. Run on the dollar causes huge loss of gold reserve at Fed, and eventual close of gold window. Oil embargo exacerbated inflation in 1973.

Collapse of tech bubble in 2000 and tragedy on 9/11 caused significant downside risk to the economy. No surprise, Fed cut interest rate in following quarters, while White House pushed to increasing housing ownership. Low rate brought a boom in housing market, and stock market alike. Recession was short, and recovery was swift. By early 2007, stock market matched the previous high set in 2000. Then, subprime mortgage market exploded, brought down Merrill, Lehman, Bear Stearns, Wachovia, Countryside, AIG, Fannie Mae and Freddie Mae...From the October '07 peak to the November 2007 low, the Dow Jones dropped 48 percent. MSCI world index lost 50% from the peak in Sep 2007. The meltdown at Wall Street rippled into global financial crisis in 2008.

Are there any systemic flaws in the global banking structure? Is central banking the savior or the culprit of those crises?

Central Banking Causes Repeated Financial Crisis

The fundamental mechanism of global banking system is based on "fractional reserve banking" (FRB). FRB works this way: when customer deposits money with a bank, the bank will keep a fraction of the deposit and can lend out the rest to other customers. The bank is required to deposit the reserve part with the central bank of the country.

Fractional reserve banking was invented by London's goldsmiths in the 16th century when London was emerging as the financial capital of Europe. Goldsmiths took deposits of gold from customers and issued deposit receipts. Customers could redeem those receipts to gold any time upon request. Shortly after, goldsmiths realized they did not have to keep all the gold deposits in their vaults, because it was unlikely that all customers would withdraw their gold deposits at the same time. They only had to keep a fraction of the deposits. By lending out the rest of gold, they could charge a fee on the gold. Over time, they realized that a reserve of 10-20% of the deposits would be adequate to meet the need of withdrawal.

That reserve ratio is still valid and close to what it is today, although the world has long abandoned gold deposits and receipts. Many countries set their reserve ratio in that range.
Assume that a central bank sets the reserve ratio at 10%. When a customer deposits 100 units of currency with a commercial bank, the bank will keep 10 as the reserve, and deposit them with the central bank.

The commercial bank can lend out the rest 90 units to a second customer. When the second customer takes the 90 units, conducts some business and then deposits the money with the bank again, the bank will keep 9 units as reserve and can lend out

81, and so on. Eventually, the initial 100 units of money will be amplified to 1,000 units, or 100/reserve ratio, of money in circulation.

If the reserve ratio was raised to 20%, the 100 unit's currency becomes 500 units in circulation. Following table illustrates the amplification of deposit, reserve and loan.

RRR=	10%		
Deposit		Reserve	Loan
100		10.0	90.0
90.0		9.0	81.0
81.0		8.1	72.9
72.9		7.3	65.6
65.6		6.6	59.0
59.0		5.9	53.1
53.1		5.3	47.8
47.8		4.8	43.0
43.0		4.3	38.7
38.7		3.9	34.9
34.9		3.5	31.4
31.4		3.1	28.2
28.2		2.8	25.4
25.4		2.5	22.9
22.9		2.3	20.6
20.6		2.1	18.5
18.5		1.9	16.7
16.7		1.7	15.0
15.0		1.5	13.5
13.5		1.4	12.2
12.2		1.2	10.9
10.9		1.1	9.8
9.8		1.0	8.9
8.9		0.9	8.0

8.0	0.8	7.2
991	**99.1**	**892.1**

There is a serious legal and regulatory issue with this banking system.

First, it changes the role of a customer from a depositor, to a debtor without the consent of the customer. When a citizen deposits his saving with a bank, he/she assumes that the bank is the safest place to put the money, and the bank keeps the money in a well-guarded vault. When the depositor needs the money, he/she can withdraw it anytime anyplace. Hence, the bank is similar to a warehouse, and money is a warehouse receipt. Although the money is homogeneous without distinction, the depositor believes that the money he/she deposited is inside the bank.

But that belief is not true.

Banks do not keep the customers' money in a safe vault. Instead, they lend the money out for a fee, exactly like the goldsmiths did. They lend the money as corporate loans, mortgage loans, and credit card loans; while they keep only a fraction of the deposit as cash to meet the withdrawal requirement.

Magically, the depositor becomes a lender to the bank for a lower yield. The bank becomes a debtor who borrows the money from the depositor, and lends the money for a higher yield.

This is a legalized embezzlement without the consent from depositors. Depositors believe that banks are operating on a 100% reserve basis, i.e. keeping all deposits in cash locked in a vault. In reality, majority of the money (1-reserve ratio) has been secretly lent out.

Goldsmiths abused the trust of customers. They did not keep the gold deposited with them in their vaults. Banks abuse the trust from depositors by lending out the money.

Irving Fisher said that 100% reserve banking was "a return from the present extraordinary and ruinous system of lending the same money 8 or 10 times over, to the conservative safety deposit system of the old goldsmiths, before they began lending out improperly what was entrusted to them for safekeeping. It was this abuse of trust that, after being accepted as standard practice, evolved into modern deposit banking. From the standpoint of public policy, it is still an abuse, no longer an abuse of trust, but an abuse of the loan and deposit functions" (Irving Fisher, *100% Money*, 1945. p18-19)

Second, this banking system is highly unstable. When business runs as usual, the reserve kept by the bank is enough to meet withdraw requirements. Banks make money by borrowing cheaply and lending expensively. Because of the mechanism of fractional reserve banking, the bank amplifies the money supply by a factor of 1/reserve ratio. If the required reserve ratio is 10%, banks can lend out 90% of the money deposited with them in any given time.

Henry C. Simons of Chicago, highly sympathetic to Fisher's view, said "we have reached a situation where private bank credit represents all but a small fraction of our total effective circulating medium. This givens us an economy in which significant disturbance of equilibrium set in motion forces which operate grossly to aggravate, rather than to correct the initial maladjustments". "our financial structure has been built largely on the illusion that funds can at the same time be both available and invested-and this observation applies to our saving banks, (and in lesser degree to many other financial institutions) as well as commercial, demand deposit banking." (Henry C Simons, *Economic Policy for a Free Society*, p55)

If all the bank's depositors decide to take 10% of their money out, the bank will run out of money. The next person in queue will be empty handed. That is what happened during the Great Depression, and during other banking crises. This is called bank-run. If you believe that your money is safe with a bank, think again.

Is there a solution to this fundamental risk of the modern banking system?

Yes, if the reserve ratio is raised to 100%. In a 100% reserve system, the bank will keep all deposited money. Banks are not allowed to lend. Banks can collect fees for safeguarding money from depositors, in a function similar to warehouses that provide storage facilities. Banks can lend their own money, but not depositors' money.

Under this system, there is no risk of bank-run, no risk of bank failures and all deposits are safe.

If this system would be so much better than the existing system, why is there no adoption? What are the incentives for building a banking system that is inherently unstable?

100% reserve banking system	Fractional reserve banking system
Banks will lose the opportunity to make most of their profits. In	In a fractional reserve bank, 100 dollars will turn into 1,000

a 100% reserve banking market, banks can make about 1% of 100 dollars, or 1 dollar.	dollars circulation money if the reserve ratio is 10%. By charging the spread of interest rates between depositors and borrowers, called net interest margin, banks make about 3% of 1,000 dollar, or 30 dollar.
Money can be created by central banks, but commercial banks can NOT leverage.	Money can be created by central banks, and commercial will amplify that money supplied. Central bank has huge capacity to change the money supply
Depositors have to pay banks a fee, say 0.4%. However, all the money deposited with the bank is safe and is always there for withdrawal.	Depositors can earn interests from their deposits. But money is not really there when depositors need it.

Bankers are the most powerful lobbyists in the world. Changing banking law to cut their profits will be fiercely fought against. In a world banking system that is well entrenched by FRB, bankers control the power, money, media and, of course, politicians

Who has the power to change banking regulation without bankers' support?

Fractional reserve banking became legalized and well entrenched worldwide since the 18th century. To perfect this unstable system, bankers needed to invent more tools to keep the systems going. No one - bankers, lawyers, professors, and the Congress, doubted or challenged the system. All students from economics department are brain-washed to worship central banking without any doubts. They all hail that central banking as the most important invention in financial history.

The role of Central Banks is to be the lender of the last resort. Through tremendous economic growth in 18th and 19th century, commercial banks in Europe experienced periodic constraint of finding money, and felt that there was not enough "elasticity" in supply. Even minor fluctuations, such as regional war, harvest, and election, could create shortage of money and bank-run, i.e. banking crisis. Many banks failed, for obvious reasons, since 18th century. During boom time, banks lend out as much as possible. Before the invention of government regulated "required reserve", banks were free to lend as they like, until a turning point that they had to face a crowd outside of their branches to withdraw money.

To fix the problem of sudden demand for liquidity, banks needed a last resort to borrow money from, when inter-bank lending was not an option, because all banks were under withdrawal pressure. That last resort was invented to provide the liquidity all banks need in a time of crisis. That lender of last resort is called the Central Bank.

History of Central Banking

A central bank has the monopoly power to create money and no other banks can issue money in any forms. Counterfeiting money is a serious criminal behavior. A central bank can create money out of air, expend credit line to commercial banks without gold or asset backup, but counterfeiting by central banks is not called "crime".

The world's first central bank, Bank of England, was established in 1694. Initially, it was the financing vehicle for King William to raise money to fight a war against France, which lasted from 1689 to 1815. By borrowing 1.2 million pound from Scottish financier, William Patterson, the bank started its operation as a commercial bank. It raised debts for the government to support war and other expenditures, and took deposits of tax money collected by the Treasury. The bank also acted to provide short-term money supply, in the form of loans, to other banks when needed.

Bank of England did not ascend to the status of a central bank until 1844 with the pass of Bank Charter Act by the Parliament, which gave exclusive note-issuing powers to the bank. At the time, Britain was under a gold exchange standard, and each pound has to be 100% backed by gold reserve at the bank. BoE had the responsibility of adjusting discount rate to manage the country's gold reserve. When discount rate was too low and loans were provided at a cheap rate, gold would flow out of BoE. When discount rate was too high, it would make fewer loans; the bank would build more reserves and bring gold back to the bank.

With the tools of loan, discount rate, and open market operation, BoE gradually mastered central banking after decades of trials and errors. For example, in 1823 to 1825, BoE set the rate too low and over-heated the economy. The bank then tightened up and caused a brief deflation.

This mechanism of adjusting discount rate was used to manage money supply, with an eventual goal of managing England's gold reserve; while nowadays, BOE adjusts the discount rate with a mission of managing inflation.

There was little to none transparency in regard to BoE's operations in the early days. Business, including banking particularly, is supposed to be separated from the government. Once questioned by the British Parliament about adequacy of its gold reserve, the Governor said that, "we have enough gold reserves. I feel uncomfortable to answer your question." Further questioned about what is enough, his answer was, "I feel very, very uncomfortable to answer that question".

In 1946, BOE was officially nationalized; and in 1971, it became an independent government agency to set monetary policy and discount rate. The ideal of separating finance from government ended. The government has been in direct control of money and finance ever since.

Federal Reserve Bank of United States was established as a private bank in 1913. Fed was established under a different ideology from that of BOE. While BOE started as a commercial bank for the King, it gradually gained the role of a central bank, which had the power of being the sole issuer of currency and being the lender of last resort. Federal Reserve System copied the model of BOE, but its function and role were debated over two decades in late 19th century. The idea of establishing a central bank for the US was promoted by some, but resisted by others.

The system resulted from struggle, compromise, and balance of the power among major interest groups, including House of Morgan from Wall Street, Rockefeller group from oil and industrial, and trade unions from regional banks. After experiencing tremendous growth as a laissez faire free market during the entire 19th century, America rose to be a world major industrial, agricultural, and financial power. Many industries, such as oil, railroad, steel, auto, have been consolidated and merged. These established big businesses wanted to sustain their profitability and stampedes competitions.

Banking industry was very fragmented at the time when every bank could issue its own notes, which served as currencies. In The Hodges Genuine Bank Notes of America (a trade directory), 1859, there were 9916 notes issued by 1356 banks. America was on a gold standard, and banks issued notes based on their gold reserves. Banks were free to issue their notes without regulations and intervention from the federal government. It was a laissez faire market for experimenting free banking ideas

Thomas Jefferson, the leading opponent of establishing a national bank, argued that banking was explicitly excluded from the power of government in Constitution. In 1863, the Federal government took control of issuing notes. National note were issued by members of the National Bank System. Those regional banks that are not part of the national banking systems were allowed to issue notes, but they have to pay 10% tax. The taxation indeed eliminated issuing of bank notes by regional banks. The US established its first national currency.

However, regional banks, particular those in St. Louis, and Chicago, flourished in the 19th century during regional economic expansion. Wall Street banks' share of deposits and bank clearance decreased significantly from 1840 to 1912. For established big Wall Street banks, they faced declining significance, and plotted to build a national cartel to re-gain control and power from regional banks. To control regional banks, the big banks, spearheaded by JP Morgan and Rockefeller, wanted a "central bank" to regulate and regional banks, to secure their own interests and to abandon gold standard eventually.

After the Civil War, economic growth skyrocket, fueled by construction and investment boom in railroad. Nevertheless, the nation's money supply was fixed precisely at $356 million of greenbacks and $300 million bank notes. There was not enough liquidity to meet the seasonal demand for money after harvesting, which along with market meltdown in Vienna, caused a panic and bank-run in September 1873. The panic added strength to the argument that US needed a central bank to provide more "elasticity" to its money supply.

It took over 20 years of interest group's lobbying, supported by newly emerged "altruistic" intellectuals, to educate American people about the benefit of having the country's banks to be regulated and managed (in time of emergency) by a central bank. The political clout to establish a central bank to provide liquidity for banks became overwhelming. Similar liquidity crisis strike again in 1907, but it was successfully resolved by J.P. Morgan, who acted like a central bank, through reducing reserves and expanding credits.

Establishing Federal Reserve Bank system finally passed Congress in 1913, and signed into law by President Woodrow Wilson. Twelve regional reserve banks were all privately owned by regional commercial banks, and stayed elusive about their ownership as of today. New York Federal Reserve Bank was the most powerful and influential one among the twelve reserve banks, led by a Morgan disciple, Benjamin Strong, until his death

146

in 1928. Like Bank of England and Bank of France, Fed has the power to be the sole issuer of currency. It was intended to be a crisis-managing bank, which would provide the liquidity to prevent panic. However that mission was soon twisted from a passive role (emergency lending) into an active role (judging the adequacy of money supply).

Even more deceptive and shrewd scheme plotted by the Fed is that central bank should to be independent of politicians, because politicians could not resist the temptation of inflation due to short election cycle. Only Fed and its private bankers are the "are among the world's fiercest inflation hawks" (**New York Times,** October 12,1993).

Why would private bankers fight against inflation? When money expands, do not banks make more profits? Whenever new money is printed, and multiplied by FRB, banks make more money by lending more to customers.

If Fed and private bankers are inflation hawks, why inflation has been much higher after Fed than that before establishing Fed?

US	GDP growth	Inflation	
1867 -1914	3.7%	0.1%	Gold standard
1929-1970	3.2%	1.5%	Gold standard
1970-2009	2.9%	4.4%	Greenback standard

Source: Federal Reserve Bank, St Louis and Angus Maddison GGDC.

Nothing should be above representative government. Is not our government "of the people, and for the people?" If politicians mess up monetary policy, or make counterfeit money, they should in jail. If the government is ruled dictator, who interferes the nation's money for his own benefits, and hence, Fed should be "independent", this government itself should be abandoned.

Shockingly, Fed is immune from Congress's scrutiny and overseeing, despite of its influence on the economy and its absolute power in supplying the money. It should be accountable for monetary results, and be completely transparent to Congress.

Thoroughly dismantle Fed Reserve banks, and return its role to Congress or Treasure, is a must-do to restore democracy in America. Establishing the central bank clearly violated Constitution, created a legalized looting of people's wealth for centuries. Indeed, it is the Fed who creates the inflation. Money printing and monetary policy should in the hands of people, represented by Congress, not decided by a secretive agency that accepts no auditing, no regulation, no budget of operation, and not appointment of officers from the Congress.

In May 1981, Friedman declared, "after studying the Fed for 67 yeas, I have no doubt that the US would be better off if the Federal Reserve had never been established." (NYDN 5/22/1981).

Inflation Is Bankers' Best Friend

With the power of loan generation, setting discount rate, and open market operation, a central bank can change the amount of money in circulation. To increase money supply, a central bank can reduce discount rate, increase loan, or buy government bonds from the market or the Treasury. After the base money being created by a central bank, the money in circulation will be amplified through fractional reserve banking.

Suppose that a central bank lends $100 to a commercial bank, or buys $100 government bond from the market, $100 new money will enter circulation. Shortly after, the $100 base money will become $1,000 on the market place if the reserve ratio is 10%. (In a real world, because not every dollar is deposited with banks, actual increase will be slightly less than $1000)

When $1,000 new money enters the circulation, merchants who sell products or service do not realize that this $1,000 is new money. People on the street do not realize any difference between new money and old money. Merchants take the money from the customers and conduct the transactions. They are happy to sell their products to the buyers. Because of those new purchases, the merchants get a boom in their business. They start to purchase more material and hire more workers. More people find jobs, and they spend their salaries on all kinds of purchases. And so on and on.

A business boom is in place. It is called the inflation boom. All governments love this monetary game to stimulate economic growth. Using fiscal policy to stimulate economy is difficult because governments have to borrow money or increase taxation. Either way is not ideal, because debt has to be paid back, and raising tax is never welcomed.

However, creating money is both subtle and effective. On the surface, everyone has more money and the economy is booming.

There is a price to be paid. This new $1,000 was not backed by gold, or goods or services created. It is solely created by the central bank. Purchase power of the entire money stock would be reduced by (1000/money stock). This is not the strict definition of inflation, but this is how inflation was originated.

Inflation is like a drug addiction for the government. At the beginning of inflationary stage, printing money creates a booming market, and politicians feel good about themselves and the economy. Indeed, that feeling good is exactly like that of taking narcotics.

The economy is in a boom. What is wrong with this money induced economic growth?

Shortly after, merchants realize that customers keep on coming. As they can not meet the demand any more, they start to raise prices. As the price goes up, their suppliers and employees realize that they can demand higher price and higher pay too. Very soon, all prices go up.

People start to realize that their money can purchase fewer goods than before because the price level has risen. They start to spend less money, and purchase fewer goods. Consumption of goods and services returns to their previous level, although price stabilizes at a higher level.

To get the economic boom going, Fed has to continue this cheating game by printing more and more money. This inflation boom is so tempting that politicians can not refuse adopting an inflationary policy. Economic professor brainwash public that growth of money should be slightly higher than GDP growth (to create >=2% inflation), when actually growth of money itself is NOT needed for economic growth.

Additionally, the government can levy more tax during the inflationary period. Because of progressive tax schedule, more income means higher marginal tax rate. Raising tax rate is never a popular move for politicians. However, by creating inflation, people will receive higher nominal salary each year. Higher income results in higher tax payment.

Also, inflation renders the government to pay back less on its debt. This is critical for a government that already owes significant public debt. Even if annual inflation is at a moderate 3%, $100 dollar principal will be eroded to $40 value, if the principal of bond is due 30 years. This is true for all debtors; inflation will reduce the value of future payments.

There is something beneficial about inflation: inflation indeed is a tax on underground economy, because inflation is a tax on entire money stock. Every dollar outstanding on the market is taxed each year by the percentage of inflation. Because underground economy is a cash economy, it is out of reach by the government to collect tax. However, underground economy can evade income tax, but not the inflation tax.

Plus, those who are home owners also benefits not only from inflation because of rising land and property prices, but also from declining mortgage value if they had borrowed at a fixed rate. Inflation will reduce the value of the outstanding mortgage they owed.

Therefore, inflation creates losers and winners. Those who win will consider the achievement a reward for their genius mind and hard work. Those who lose will consider that the society treats them unfairly and they will try to retaliate. When the inflation reaches an extreme level, social unrest can happen.

Sir Otto Niemeyer, financial controller at the Treasury and a director at the Bank of England, wrote a memorandum to Churchill that:

"You can by inflation (a most vicious form of subsidy) enable temporary spending power to cope with large quantities of products. But unless you increase the dose continually there comes a time when having destroyed the credit of the country you can inflate no more, money having ceased to be acceptable as a value. Even before this, as your inflated spending creates demand, you have had claims for increased wages, strikes, lockouts, etc. I assume it will be admitted that with Germany and Russia before us (runaway inflation) we do not think plenty can be found on this path."

Banks are forever tempted by inflation boom, which means more deposits and more lending. However, we are repeatedly told that it is the central banker that keeps inflation in control and private bankers "are among the world's fiercest inflation hawks". Actually, the central bank creates inflation.

"The public, in the mythology of the Fed and its supporters, is a great beast, continually subject to a lust for inflating the money supply and therefore for subjecting the economy to inflation and its dire consequences. Those dreaded all-too-frequent inconveniences called "elections" subject politicians to these temptations, especially in political institutions such as the House of Representatives who come before the public every two years and are therefore particularly responsive to the public will. The Federal Reserve, on the other hand, guided by monetary experts independent of the public's lust for inflation, stands ready at all times to promote the long-run public interest by manning the battlements in an eternal fight against the Gorgon of inflation. The public, in short, is in desperate need of absolute control of money by the Federal Reserve to save it from itself and its short-term lusts and temptations."(Source: Murray N. Rothbard, *A History of Money and Banking in the US)*

How can that be true? We just analyzed how money is created, and how the central bank creates inflation. Issuing debt and collecting tax by the government do not increase money supply, because they only change the ownership the money. Only the central bank has the power and the tool to change money supply. When government issues debts, central bank buys them by writing a check or simply debits that amount of money on the Treasury's cash account. Money is hence created from air, and transferred from one pocket to another.

"If the chronic inflation undergone by Americans, and in almost every other country, is caused by the continuing creation of new money, *and if* in each country it's governmental "Central Bank" (in the United States, the Federal Reserve) is the sole monopoly source and creator of all money, *who then* is responsible for the blight of inflation? Who except the very institution that is solely empowered to create money, that is, the Fed (and the Bank of England, and the Bank of Italy, and other central banks) *itself?"*(Source: Murray Rothbard, *Case Against the Fed*)

When inflation is high, not necessary hyperinflation, government faces the danger of losing credibility and causing revolts. When a government cannot tax further on its citizen, it always resorts to issuing more money, either by devaluing its coins under gold standard, or by printing more paper money.

And subsequent inflation only makes the situation worse.

The same story has been repeated again and again; Roman emperors inflated by reducing gold and silver contents in coins; Germany Weimar Republic printed so much money that the paper was worth less than its value as fuel; China nationalist regime in 1940s replaced silver coin with paper money so that supply was no longer constrained.

Repeatedly, hyperinflation resulted in revolt and war, and many governments were thrown out because they devalued the money and ruined people's life. If the inflation is such a bad thing, why would all politicians be so addicted to it? Have they read any history books and known that inflation destroyed empires and collapsed governments?

"We are now so conditioned by permanent price inflation that the idea of prices *falling* every year is difficult to grasp. And yet, prices generally fell every year from the beginning of the Industrial Revolution in the latter part of the eighteenth century until 1940, with the exception of periods of major war, when the governments inflated the money supply radically and drove up prices, after which they would gradually fall once more. We have to realize that falling prices did not mean depression, since costs were falling due to increased productivity, so that profits were not sinking."(Source: Murray Rothbard, *A History of Money and Banking in the US*)

What Happened in 1929, 1973, and 2008

The stock market crashed in those years. Many books and research papers have discussed the cause of those crashes - greedy speculators, oil shocks, unions, careless bank lending as culprits. Those reasons might be relevant, but they were peripheral, certainly did not identify the root cause.

Rarely mentioned were the governments and central banks' role in the market crashes. What has Fed done prior to the start of trouble?

The world financial markets in 1920s were heavily instrumented and masterfully maneuvered by two figures - Benjamin Strong, the governor of Federal Reserve Bank of New York, and Bank of England's Governor, Montagu Norman. Strong was a close ally of JP Morgan, which profited tremendously during the World War I as the sole supplier of military goods to Britain and France. Once appointed in 1914, Strong immediately advocated the "international central bank cooperation", which implied structured and synchronized inflation. His strong grip of power and influence rendered the New York Fed, not the Board of Federal Reserve Bank system in Washington, the decision maker of American monetary policy. He stayed in the position till his death in 1928.

Immediately after the war, Britain intended to return the old value of sterling pound and restore gold standard, without giving up its inflationary policy, which was in place to avoid an export-induced recession. This contradictory goal was seemingly impossible to achieve. But the genius mind of Montagu Norman, aided by altruistic Strong, achieved that goal at the expense of America's and many other countries' interests. Montagu Norman was always secretive and was rarely seen in social circles, except his annual vacation time with Strong.

The core of their strategy was to inflate the dollar so that pound could restore its value of $4.86. (Post war 1 pound = $3.20, $1=1/20 ounce of gold) Under a secret agreement with Bank of England, from 1917 to 1925, Fed engaged very inflationary monetary policy. By keeping the interest rate low, Strong generated huge credit expansion, which depreciated the dollar so that pound could return to $4.86 from the $3.20 post war level. *The Banker* of London, hailed Strong as "the one the best friends England ever had."

By returning to a gold exchange standard, Sterling Pound actually became the reserve currency for European countries, i.e. central banks of those countries hold pound as the reserve, not gold. Pound was redeemable to gold bullion at Bank of England by foreign central banks.

Based on this pyramid structure of currencies, Britain could increate the supply of pound and inflated its economy; and rest of the world inflated on top of pound. Cheap money became a global phenomenon.

History is the best testimony. Discount rate at the New York Fed was reduced gradually from 7% in January 1921 to 3.5% in January 1925. The discount rate stayed at 3.5-4.0% range till late 1928. (Source: Milton Friedman, *A Monetary History,* p282)

Under this inflationist's Fed, the stock boomed with Dow Jones climbing from 71 in September 1921 to 380 in 1929. Total return during the period was 435%.

In July 1927 in New York, at a secret central banks conference, Benjamin Strong, the governor of New York Federal, told the French representative that he would give "a little coup de whiskey to the stock market". (Notice Biographique, p1005, Charles Rist, 1955). In late 1927, Strong not only reduced rate further, but also massively increased purchasing of government securities by $445 million.

After New York Fed raised rate from 3.5% in 1925 to 6% in 1929, speculative run of stock market finally ended in Sep 1929. Dow Jones dropped 47%, from 381 in Sep 1929, to 200 in Nov 1929. And market continued its free fall to the lowest of 42 in July 1932, a shocking loss of 89% from the peak of the market.

The fall in stock price and tightening of credit condition caused severe recession, rising unemployment and hardship for millions American. Middle class and farmers lost their jobs, savings, land and houses from their hard work for generations. Great Depression spread to Europe and other regions, and caused a global disaster.

In April 1933, President Roosevelt issued executive order to confiscate all the gold owned by American citizens. All citizens had to sell their gold coins, and jewelry to the government at official price of $20.67/ounce. This has been the value of the dollar since the foundation of the United States when dollar became the currency. (The initial value of the dollar was defined as $18.65/ounce since 1792 and was slightly devalued to $20.67/ounce in 1835. (Nathan Lewis: *Gold-The Once and Future Money*, p156)

After the confiscation, Roosevelt devalued the dollar to $35/ounce. This confiscation, in the name of national emergency, was probably the biggest robbery in human history. (The law was not lifted till 1975).

The Federal Reserve Bank and the Treasury Department engineered this disaster!

The stock market crashed in 1973. S&P 500 lost 38% from Dec 1972 to Oct 1974. Indeed, the market was dismal for more than a decade. After S&P 500 reaching 108 in Dec 1968, the market went through huge swings and stayed in that level for over 14 years. Inflation exceeded double digits in 1974-1975 and 1979-1981 and was in high single digit continuously for most of the decade.

Annual inflation exceeded double digits in recent history during only 3 periods, which were World War I, World War II, and 1970s. Fiscal spending and high inflation during war times were easy to justify. Inflation was much higher during America Revolution and Civil War, both financed by printing paper money. Not surprisingly, inflation in 1970s shared same causes - loose monetary policy, huge spending on Vietnam War, Medicare, and Great Society programs.

Government budge deficits soared in 1960s and 1970s. During the years of fighting the Vietnam War, the annual defense spending averaged $300 billion from 1955-1975. Defense cost was a heavy burden on the society. Fighting wars on several foreign fronts and spending domestically on the "Great Society" programs by President Lyndon Johnson would only mean one thing to the Treasury Department - borrow and spend. As government spent more money than tax revenue, more debt were accumulated.

Since 1965, US government was on deficits each and every year, from modest $1.4 billion in 1965 to $212 billion in 1985. Those deficits had to be financed by debt issuing from the Dept of Treasury. Government debt rose from $317 billion in 1965 to $1,823 billion in 1985.

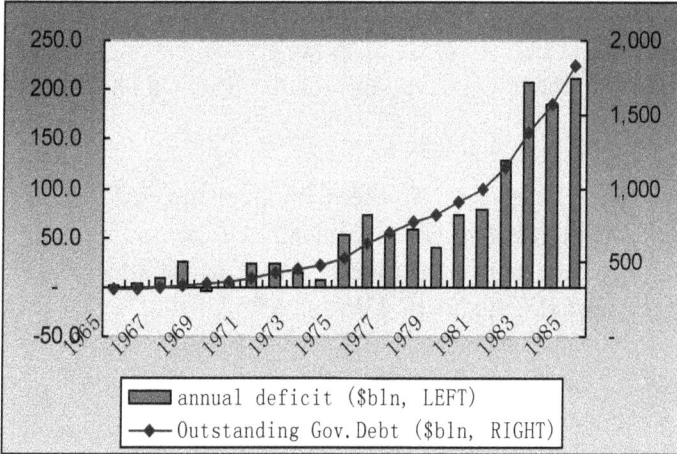

Source: Congressional Budget Office, Dept of Treasury, Federal Reserve Bank

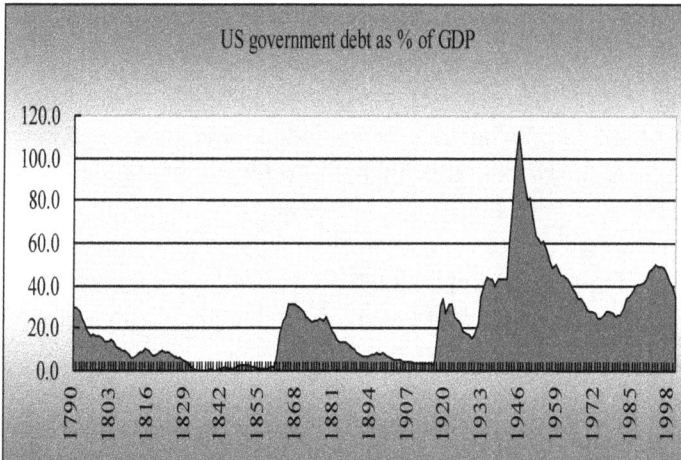

Source: Congressional Budget Office, Dept of Treasury, Federal Reserve Bank

Not surprisingly, in order to reduce borrowing cost, Fed kept the rate low. This low rate, around 5%, sustained for the most part of the Vietnam War period (1955-1975). Only after the inflation pop up significantly, Fed was forced to raise rate. By then, the Fed was already behind the curve, and inflation was on a runaway train.

Starting from 1979, when Paul Volker took over the Fed, he raised interest rates to tame down the inflation. The Fed raised overnight lending rate from 6.6% in Dec 1977, to 10% in Dec 1978, 13.8% in Dec 1979, and 19% in Jan 1981.

Inflation, which peaked at 13.5% in 1981, was successfully lowered to 3.2% by 1983.

Thanks to the tight Fed policy, inflation was back to 4% range in 1986. (Paul Volcker retired from the Fed in 1987) Higher interest rate broke the wage-price spiral, but caused severe recession and higher unemployment. However, this was the medicine that America had to take to cure the inflation disease - extravagant spending and heavy borrowing in previous years. "I do not know of any example of any inflation that has been ended without an interim period of slow economic growth and higher than usual unemployment" (Milton Friedman, Money Mischief, p222).

There is no evidence that central banks achieved the goal of "maximum employment, stable prices, and moderate long-term interest rates."

It is the 21st century. By now, central banks should have learned lessons and mastered central banking. Nevertheless, the conclusion from those history lessons is that central banks did NOT reduce business cycle. Indeed, tempted constantly by inflation boom, central banks created repeated inflation booms, and subsequent economic recessions, i.e. exacerbated business cycles.

Business cyclicality was low during Greenspan years by many measures. The country entered a "new paradigm" with low rate, and low inflation, partly because of gain of productivity and globalization. Low rate and low inflation made money easily available everywhere in the world. American prosperity seemed to have no ending. All of this sounded exactly likes what President Coolidge and Treasury Secretary Mellon said in 1927.

Suddenly, in 2008, the most severe stock market correction and financial crisis in history hit the nation. S&P 500 fell by 57% from Oct 2007 to March 2009. It started with a problem called subprime mortgage lending, which meant banks lend money to people who could not afford the houses they purchased. It was no surprise that banks, which held or traded those mortgage assets, went into bankruptcy. On the list were Bear Stearns, Lehman Brothers, AIG, Wachovia, Countryside, and Merrill Lynch; and across the Atlantic, RBS, Barclays, Fortis, HBOS, Northern Rock.

What caused this global financial crisis?

Well, the same old story was repeated. We had the tech bubble in the 90s when Internet startups were red hot, just as those railway and steel stocks in 1920s, and radio and electronics companies in 1960s. Every generation had its nifty-fifty stocks. After the tech bubble burst and the tragedy on 9/11, the global economy was heading to a downturn, which seemed inevitable.

Then, came the magic rate cut from the Fed.

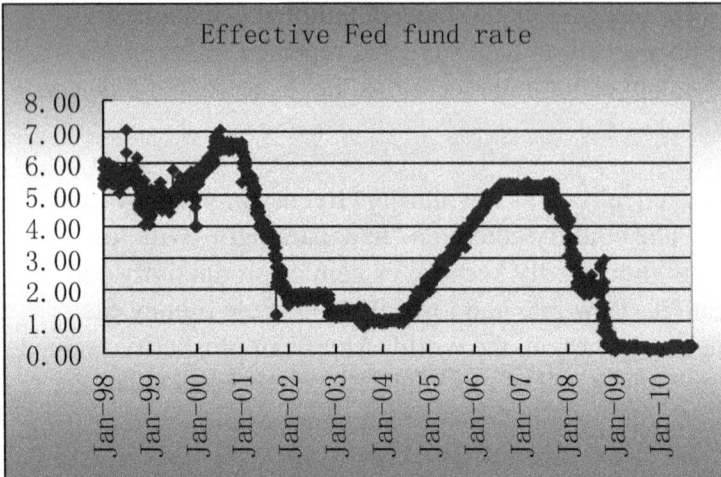

Source: Fed Res Bank of St. Louis

Fed fund rate was reduced from 6% in 2001 to 1.5% in early 2002, far below the long term average of 5%. The rate stayed in that level for years. (Fed fund rate briefly was raised to 5-6% in 2006-2007, but was reduced to an unprecedented low since 2009. As of year end 2010, the rate was about 0.2 %)

During this period, the US engaged in the Gulf War to oust Saddam Hussein out of Kuwait, and then in the Iraq War since 2003. To finance those two wars, Treasury issued more debts to finance budge deficits each year.

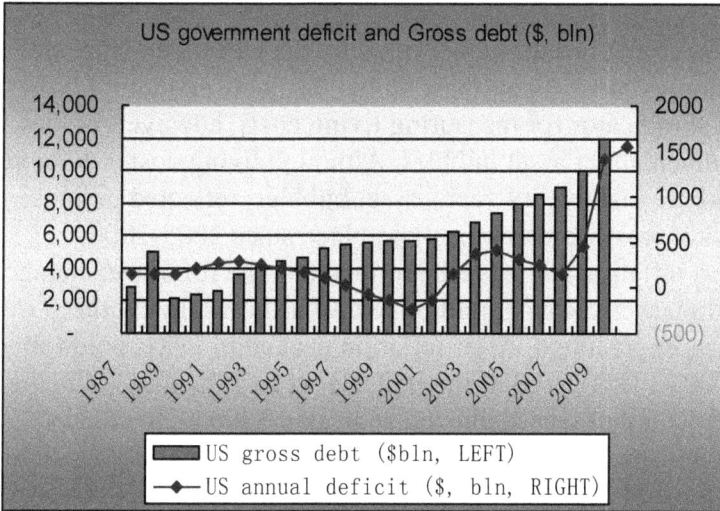

US government deficit and Gross debt ($, bln)

Source: Dept of Treasury, CBO.

The low rate and loose mortgage lending together created unprecedented booming house market. many blamed careless lenders, speculative homeowners, clueless fund managers, and greedy Wall Street bankers for 2008 financial crisis. However, they could not create this colossal bubble without "low rate". If the rate were not so low, homeowners would not have refinanced or borrowed. If the Fed had taken a moderate monetary policy post 9/11, there would have been no housing bubble and no 2008 crisis.

Although, there were many warnings about the health of the United States economy, many economists and analysts believed that "this time is different". Globalization and technology were hailed for the gain in productivity and for the global boom. In this new paradigm, why should we worry about asset bubble and inflation? With low rate and full employment, wasn't this the dream scenario that all politicians want?

In the meantime, inflation, measured by the CPI index, appeared almost non-existent. Economist hailed the "new economy". CPI is a useful indicator for measuring living costs, however, it does not tell much about asset bubbles. Although living cost did not go up quickly in last twenty years, asset bubbles, reflected in house and stock prices, were obviously in place since 2005-2006. However, inflation started to be reflected in the foreign exchange and gold markets. Rising gold price told us how quickly the dollar was depreciated. After inflation peaked in 1981, gold fell from $700 in 1980 to $320 in 1982. Between 1981 and 2005, the value of the dollar was stabilized at around $400/ounce for 14 years. Since 2005, the dollar took a nosedive from $400/ounce to $880 at the end of 2008. At the end of 2010, dollar was valued at about $1390/ounce.

Global stock markets boomed after burst of tech bubble in 2000. MSCI World index, which measures 25 country's stock market on a capitalization weighted basis, returned 153% from 2004 to 2007. When the music stopped in 2008, all those booms went bust. Overvalued stocks, houses, commodities, and golf courses, took a big downturn. It is obvious that the cheap dollar was the ultimate culprit. Inflationist from Washington created the boom and bust cycle again and again.

In September 1976, Prime Minister James Callaghan of Britain said, "we used to think that you could just spend your way out of a recession and increase employment by cutting taxes and boosting government spending. I tell you in all candour that that option no longer exists; and that insofar as it ever did exist, it only worked by injecting bigger doses of inflation into the economy followed by higher levels of unemployment as the next step. That is the history of the past twenty years."

Fed accomplished only one thing for American people - print money and devalue dollar. Did the Fed state that its goal is to keep price level stable? Well, dollar has been devalued from $20/ounce of gold in the 1914 when Fed was founded, to $1390/ounce in 2010.

What were the consequences of Fed's super elites managing our money?

	1929	1973	2008
Monetary policy	Fed conducted very loose monetary policy to reduce the value of Dollar so that British Pound could return to gold standard at pre-World War I level. This low rate and cheap dollar policy sustained for most of 1920s.	Nixon's expansionary monetary policy resulted in a flood of dollar on the international market. European central banks redeemed huge amount of gold from the Fed. Rate was kept low for most of time in late 60s. Abandoned gold standard in 1971 so that America could indefinitely increases its money supply.	Post 9/11, Fed reduced rate from 6% in 2001 to 1% in 2002 and kept it low for years. This loose monetary policy caused a huge wave of home refinancing and new mortgage lending. After exhausting the pool of people to refinance, banks started to lend money to those who could not afford purchasing houses.

Fiscal policy and War	Fiscal policy did not have significant impacts during the period.	Rising budget deficits due to Vietnam war and Great Society spending. Using ever-expanding government deficits and national debts to finance Medicare, Medicaid, moon landing etc.	Gulf War in 1990, Iraq war in 2003, in addition to other spending, caused skyrocketing federal budget deficits.

| No impact | Inflation was already high in early 70s. Above 5% in 70 and 71. On Aug 15, 1971, Nixon announced price control. The program was terminated in April 1974. According to economist Robert J. Gordon, inflation was tame temporarily during Aug 71 and Apr 74. However, inflation rocked back after price control was lifted, and reached a level in 3Q75 that it would have been, had been no price control. Cheap oil ended in 1973, and oil shock drove up the headline inflation. | "One factor, which illustrates my point about the adaptability and flexibility of the U.S. economy, is the pronounced decline in the energy intensity of the economy since the 1970s. Since 1975, the energy required to produce a given amount of output in the United States has fallen by about half. This great improvement in energy efficiency was less the result of government programs than of steps taken by households and businesses in response to higher energy prices, including substantial investments in more energy-efficient equipment and means of transportation. This improvement in energy efficiency is one of the reasons |

Job loss	Unemployment rate 25%	Unemployment 9% job loss in 1973= 3 million	Unemployment rate=10% In 2008, the number of jobs lost =2.6 million.
	In 1927, President Coolidge announced that the US was in a "new era of perpetual prosperity" and permanently rising stock price. On Nov 16, 1927, the New York Times declared that the administration in Washington was the source of most of the bullish news and noted that growing "impressions that Washington may be depended upon to furnish a fresh impetus for the stock market." In March 1929, Coolidge called American prosperity "absolutely sound" and assured everyone that stocks were	When "everyone needs a computer was the investment catching statement, tech stocks were darlings of the stock market. Valuations of IBM, EDS, Intel, Apple, Texas Instrument, reached unprecedented level; Average PE of tech stocks were 114, with many of companies generating no cash flow and earnings. McDonalds and Disney traded at PE over 70x forward earnings. Time magazine reported on Jan 8th, 1973, just 3 days before the crash, that 1973 was "shaping up as a gilt-edged year". After the crash of the	Fed and its followers advocated that a new paradigm in economic growth of US, driven by productivity gain and less dependence on commodity. "Productivity gains in the United States have been exceptional in recent years. But, for a country already on the cutting edge of technology to maintain this pace for a protracted period into the future would be without modern precedent. (Greenspan, Aug

	"cheap at current prices" (source: Ibid p116-117. and Commercial and Financial Chronicle, 4/20/1929, p2557)	market, IBM stayed flat from 1968 to 1993.	27, 2004)
Boom	Dow Jones climbing from 71 in Sep 1921 to 380 in 1929. Total return during the period was 435% (CAGR was 23%).	S&P 500 climbed from 57 in 1963 to 116 in 1972. Stock market did not perform well in 1970s. There was no obvious market bubble.	S&P zoomed from 800 in 2002 to 1280 in June 2008. Valuation started to look expensive.
Bust	Dow Jones dropped 47%, from 381 in Sep 1929, to 200 in Nov 1929. And market continued its free fall to the low of 42 in July 1932, a shocking loss of 89% from the peak of the market.	From the peak in January '73 to the low in December '74, the Dow Jones lost 46%. S&P 500 lost 36% during the same period.	From the October '07 peak to the November 2007 low, the Dow Jones dropped 48 percent. MSCI world index lost 50% from the peak in Sep 2007.

Consequence	Confiscated gold holding and devalued dollar from $20 to $35/ounce.	Entirely de-monetized gold. Unilaterally abandoned Bretton Woods's agreement, which was the core of post war global monetary system. The Fed over-supplied dollar to the international markets and lost more than half of its gold reserve. Dollar devalued from $35/ounce gold in 1971 to $614/ounce in 1980.	Quantitative easing doubled the Fed's balance sheet, increased the dollar in the circulation, although most of the new money supplies were not in the form of high-powered M0 money. Dollar devalued from $409/ounce in 2004 to $1390 in 2010.

To What Degree Will Dollar Devalue

After the 2008 financial crisis, global central banks took the opportunity to print money on a scale dwarfed all monetary expansions in history. By cutting discount rate, buying financial assets, and providing extra credit line to banks, money to run US economy, in abstract concept, has been quadrupled! While the size of GDP stayed about the same as pre-crisis.

On October 3rd, 2008, Bush approved the $300 billion TARP (troubled assets relief program) plan to alleviate US banks from toxic assets. The program authorized Department of Treasury purchasing or insuring assets from banks up to $700 billion. And on October 14th, the US government revised the plan, allowing TARP money to buy banks' preferred stocks.

On December 23rd 2008, the European Union approved 500 billion pound, 120 billion euro aid package for financial institutions. The Federal Reserve Board announced on February 10, 2009 that it was prepared to undertake a substantial expansion of the TALF (Term ABS Loan Facility). The expansion could increase the size of the TALF to as much as $1 trillion. On February 13 2009, the US announced a $787 billion, the largest ever, fiscal stimulus plan.

On December 16 2008, Fed reduced fed fund rate to 0-0.25% range. On January 8th 2009, the Bank of England reduced discount rate to 1.5%, the lowest in BOE's history. All those preemptive measures might be "effective" in saving banks, which seemed to be the main mandate of Fed; But the moral hazards of quantitative easing, potential in creating asset bubbles, and eventual hyper-inflation will be far-reaching and dangerous! Alan Greenspan commented in an article "Inflation Is The Big Threat To A Sustained Recovery" on June 26, 2009 *Financial*

Times that, "the US is faced with the choice of either paring back its budget deficits and monetary base as soon as the current risks of deflation dissipate, or setting the stage for a potential upsurge in inflation"

Fed's balance sheet demonstrated how much money had been created by the central bank since 2008. By reducing Fed fund rate to almost zero, plus quantitative easing, Fed has created about $1,400 billion by 2011! (Source: Federal Reserve Bank of St Louis)

let's calculate how low the dollar will go by looking at money velocity. The quantity theory of money says that: $M \times V = P \times Y$
Where
M= amount of money
V= velocity of money
P= price level
Y=annual production.

Total output, Y, is relatively constant (recession was shallow, and growth was slow). If the velocity is kept at a stable level, the amount of money will determine the price level. If money in circulation is doubled, price level will increase proportionally. Because the Fed' liability side expanded by more than twice, if other factors held constant, price should be doubled.

Hence, inflation should be around 100%, or gold price at about $2000/ounce. However, the collapse of money velocity offset the increase of money and credits Fed created. Those credit lines created by the Fed for Treasury and banks were not immediately used, similar to a new credit card that a consumer received but not used.

Over time, when Treasury uses that money to pay for the stimulus programs, money will gradually roll out from the Treasury. The reserve bank credits were created when the Fed swapped commercial banks' securities holdings, particular MBS, with cash, so that banks could be relieved from the pressure of falling MBS prices. The cash received by banks stayed on their balance sheet, with very little being lent out. On the Fed's liability side, currency in circulation remained relatively flat. When Treasury and banks start to use those cash and credits they are currently holding or saving with the Fed, money supply will more than double and inflation will flare up.

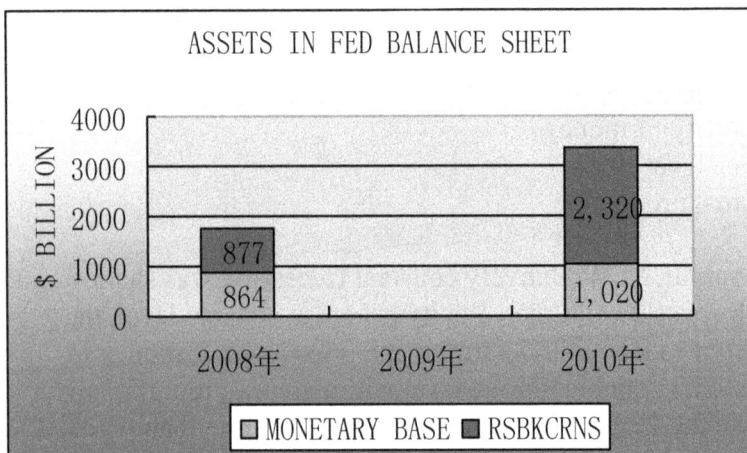

ASSETS IN FED BALANCE SHEET

	2008年	2009年	2010年
RSBKCRNS	877		2,320
MONETARY BASE	864		1,020

$ BILLION — 0, 1000, 2000, 3000, 4000

☐ MONETARY BASE ■ RSBKCRNS

Source: Federal Reserve Bank

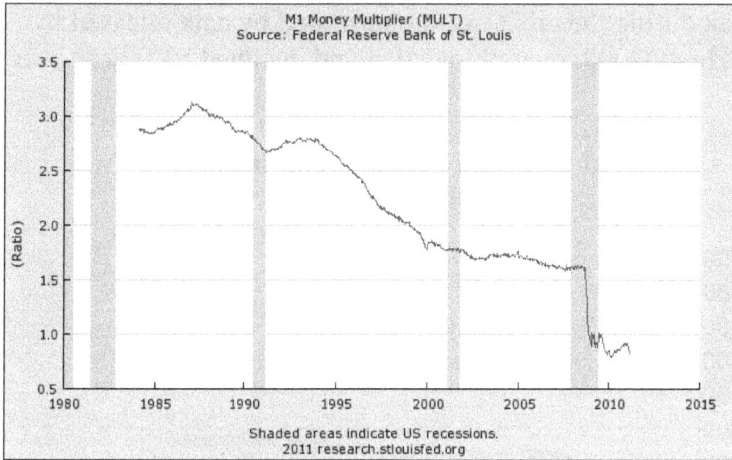

Source: Federal Reserve Bank of St. Louis

The US base money expanded meaningfully, from $864 billion in June 2008, to $1020 billion in June 2010, 18% increase in two years. The increase of base money was above the long-term average of 6%. The increased base money, which is the most powerful form of money, was offset by the declining money multiplier. Money multiplier is the factor that amplifies base money to the amount of money in circulation.

Money multiplier = (cu+1) / (cu+rr)
Money supply = (cu+1) / (cu+rr) x Base money
Where cu = cash/deposit, and rr = reserve/deposit

Based on H8 report from the Fed, which provides the "Assets and Liabilities of Commercial Banks in the United States" ($ billion), what we can see is that nearly half of the money, $700 billion approximately, provided by the Fed's expansion of balance sheet, stayed on the balance sheet of commercial banks! Commercial banks were so fearful of risks, that they were not willing to lend, and rather kept all that cash on the balance sheet, buy government bonds, or deposited it with the Fed as reserves. Loan demand was weak during the crisis, as demonstrated by data released by the Fed. In 4Q2008, overall loan demand declined 53% year over year.

Cash held by all US commercial banks ($million)

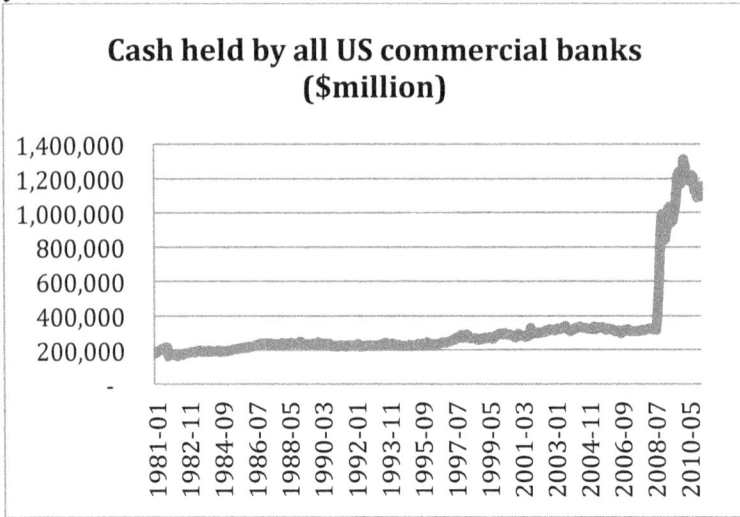

Source: Federal Reserve Bank of St. Louis

This explanation was well supported by the St Louis Fed's data; falling money multiplier offset the increased monetary base, which partially explained the lack of inflation in the market place. When banks are confident enough to use the reserve at the central bank to lend, money supply will increase significantly. Overall, the liquidity on the market remained adequate, but not excessive. The danger of future inflation can flare up, if the money multiplier returns to its normal level.

St Louis Adjusted Monetary Base (Solid Line)   M1 Money Multiplier (Dashed Line)

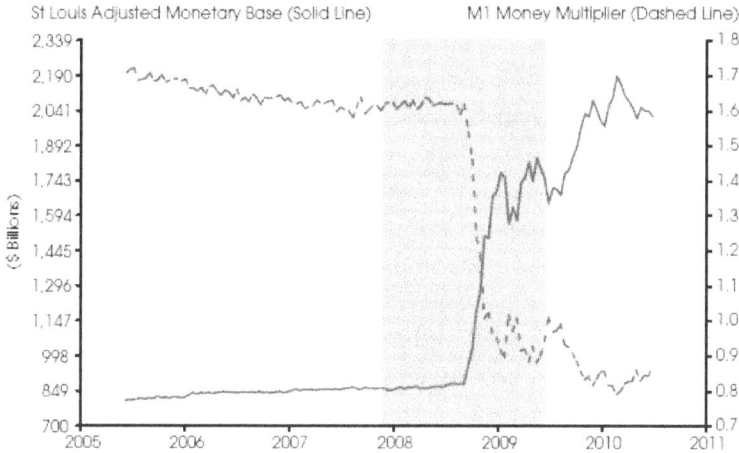

NOTE: The shaded area indicates the most recent U.S. recession.

Source: St. Louis Fed

If the value of dollar is to be halved in a five-year period, inflation will reach 14% on an annual average. If that happens in a seven-year period, annual inflation will be around 10%. Indeed, the rising gold price, from $880 in 2008 to $1390 in 2010, already reflected the market's expectation about the value of dollar and inflation. If the monetary easing is fully reflected, gold should trade around $2000. However, Fed can drain liquidity out of the system, and hence, keep inflation at a low single digit level. The Fed is not static.

In following years, inflation can exceed double digits and the dollar may lose half its value. If the Fed acts quickly enough and drains the excess liquidity out of the economy, inflation target of 1-3% may be achieved, and Fed's balance sheet may return to its pre-crisis normal level, which means, "stealing" people's wealth at a slower pace, so that there are no social unrests on the street.

"I know no example in history of a substantial inflation lasting for more than a brief time that was not accompanied by a roughly corresponding rapid increase in the quantity of money; and no example of a rapid increase in the quantity of money that was not accompanied by a roughly correspondingly substantial inflation" (Friedman, *Money Mischief*, p195)

Fed is the lobbying agency of a cartel group disguised as a government agency. Its mandate is to protect a banking system that maximizes banks' profits, while camouflage itself as a government agency so that its credibility, control, and real mission are NOT challenged and revealed. After establishing Fed, American economy has grown at slower pace with higher inflation, and Fed indeed fulfilled its real mission – enrich the few elite and loot the public wealth, through inflation and repeated crisis.

By completely dismantling the Fed system, and returning the power of money printing to the Congress, American democracy and economy can sustain and flourish. Dollar has devalued from being equivalence of 1/18.65 ounce of gold to 1/1200 ounce of gold in over two hundred forty years. Astronomical number of wealth has been confiscated and stolen from the public in the form of inflation. Gold standard is the roadblock to create inflation, and hence has been ridiculed and despised by elite "experts" and "economists". Establishing Fed and abandoning gold revolutionized money creation, and provided infinite potential to devalue the dollar.

When greenback is devalued to newspaper, and top 1% has all the wealth, our democracy is under threat, and our beloved Republic is in danger!

CHAPTER 7 - Create Jobs In Old Fashion
– Build the Border Wall, Highway and Airport!

Feb 18th, 2008, Milwaukee, Wisconsin. Then would-be First Lady Michelle Obama said, "for the first time in my adult life I am proud of my country because it feels like hope is finally making a comeback." Then in Madison, Wis, later that day, she said, "For the first time in my adult lifetime, I'm really proud of my country, and not just because Barack has done well, but because I think people are hungry for change."

Dec 19th 2016, Michele told Oprah Winfrey in an interview inside White House, aired on CBS, "We feel the difference now. See, now, we are feeling what not having hope feels like," "Hope is necessary. It's a necessary concept and Barack didn't just talk about hope because he thought it was just a nice slogan to get votes. He and I and so many believe that -- what else do you have if you don't have hope. What do you give your kids if you can't give them hope?"

Hope Begins When Obama Move Out Of White House!

Jan 20, 2017 was a day to remember in history when Obama moved out of White House. Obama's Presidency was a total failure. He failed to deliver economic growth, to create job and brought the nation to edge of bankruptcy. He ruined America's confidence, superiority and leadership in the world.

From their own voices, as Michele admitted, million American lost their no hope due to his total failure. Lack of hope was a true, accurate reflection of American society during Obama's eight years in White House. Indeed, it was the darkest time in American history. Obama accomplished absolute nothing except that American continued to lose million manufacturing job, except that America lost military superiority and failed in Iraq, Afghanistan and Syria, except that Obama spent millions dollars on vacation and global traveling. America lost respects from friends and foes. At an international conference on climate change, a foreign official even pointed finger at Obama's face.

The shockingly sad truth of Obama's failure is countless. But the media, controlled by Democrats and interest groups, is still fooling Americans with false economic data and praises of achievements. Those lies are absolutely outrageous and shameless. A few number checks (based on government statistics!) demonstrate how disastrous his Presidency was from 2008 to 2016.

1. People collecting food stamp rose from 28 million to 44 million
2. Mass shooting increased from 8 (Bush's 8 years) to 162
3. National debt rose from $10 trillion to $19 trillion
4. Real household income declined 2.3%

GDP growth during Obama time, at 1.6% annually, was the slowest among 13 Presidents since 1945. More shockingly, at the same time, national debt increased by $9 trillion, which nearly doubled all debts accumulated over previous 240 years in America history!

How could he fail the US economy so badly? With this type of economic performance and debt accumulation, should he be locked in jail forever? Where did the money go?

It is difficulty to figure out how did he waste or steal billions from Americans. (DOJ is investigating potential abuse of billions dollars funding to some Obama's inner circle friends' NGO). Nevertheless, even based on Congress budget figures, it is easy to see Obama's outrageous spending! Hand out Food stamps, expand federal agencies, build museums, fund NGOs, reward his friends with bogus contracts, and spend $100 million on travel!

Obama campaigned to reduce "economic injustice". Obama said in 2012 re-election campaign trail that, "This is a make-or-break moment for the middle Class. I believe that this country succeeds when everyone gets a fair shot." It is true that a healthy society prefer big part of people in the middle category. But if everyone is equal in economic interest, that society is called communism. After 50 years of civil rights movement, American is already half way on a communist path, and Obama campaigned to complete that transformation. Fortunately, he failed, and failed terribly.

Did he close the income gap? And helped his voters climbing economic ladder? Ironically, the answer is NO. The gap actually expanded, reached the highest level since 1920s. And lower income population was worse than after his eight years in office. Lack of hope? Blame Obama.

However, he did handout nice perks to his supporters – included in the 2009 stimulus package, one thing particularly shockingly was the $21 billion food stamps! Does he really think putting people on food stamp can help economic recovery? When do those people after finishing their beer and burger? They need more, and much more (and free medicine too).

Obama conducted the biggest robbery of middle class Americans in history! The stimulus package was only a beginning. His huge deficit budget spending, each and every year, were full of dirty, wasteful, filthy items that stole billions and billions from tax-paying, law-abiding, real Americans.

If the package had dedicated on infrastructure building instead of welfare giving, millions job would have been created that instantaneously pull the country out of recession. Out of $787 billion, only $17 billion was spend on rail transportation and public transit (food stamp was $21 billion!), at a time when our airport and highway has degraded into 3rd world condition (as Joe Biden famously claimed).

If we had build a new subway for NYC, or a tunnel upgrade, or a new bridge, the multiplier effects from those projects would be extremely effective in creating jobs – jobs in design and engineering, in steel and cement production, in construction, and in food services and financial services etc.

Even more ridiculously, tax cut for business? $41 million (out of a 787 billion package)

As discussed in chapter 1, because of lower corporate tax rate in overseas, corporate America kept their foreign earnings in overseas entities. At the time of 2009, this number was estimated to be over $700 billion (and rose to $2 trillion in 2016). Had corporate tax rate being cut, those funds would have been repatriated, and created stimulus that was more powerful than the government stimulus plan. A recovery would not need a penny from taxpayer, and would not add a penny to the national debt!

Waste from this stimulus is beyond counting, and made American beyond being angry. All those spending had added to our national debt, and had to be paid by future generations.

Outburst of anger was only inevitable!

President Obama, Are You Listening?

(Following were from CNBC transcript, Feb 20, 2009)
RICK SANTELLI: The government is promoting bad behavior.
Because we certainly don't want to put stimulus forth and give
people a whopping $8 or $10 in their check, and think that they
ought to save it, and in terms of modifications... I'll tell you what,
I have an idea. You know, the new administration's big on
computers and technology-- How about this, President and new
administration? Why don't you put up a website to have people
vote on the Internet as a referendum to see if we really want to
subsidize the losers' mortgages; or would we like to at least buy
cars and buy houses in foreclosure and give them to people that
might have a chance to actually prosper down the road, and
reward people that could carry the water instead of drink the
water?
TRADER ON FLOOR: That's a novel idea. (Applause, cheering)
JOE KERNEN: Hey, Rick... Oh, boy. They're like putty in your
hands. Did you hear...?
SANTELLI: No they're not, Joe. They're not like putty in our
hands. This is America! How many of you people want to pay for
your neighbor's mortgage that has an extra bathroom and can't
pay their bills? Raise their hand. (Booing) ***President Obama, are***
you listening?"
The 2009 stimulus plan was Obama "thank you" handout to his
supporters. Why no cut of corporate tax, no infrastructure
building, and no effort in reduction of trade deficit? Because
American in those industries were not Obama's constituency!
The plan had little impact on US economy. It was a moral and
economic hazard that led to social division and anger. In Feb
2009, famed and respected economist Larry Kudlow
supported the protest of Tea party on the stimulus plan: "Team
Obama is rewarding bad behavior. It is enlarging moral hazard. It
is expanding its welfarist approach to economic policy. And with

a huge expansion of government-owned zombie lenders Fannie Mae and Freddie Mac, Team Obama is taking a giant step toward nationalizing the mortgage market. . ."

Things got worse and worse as Obama stayed in White House. According to USDA data, people received supplemental nutritional assistance rose from 28 million in 2008, to 44 million in 2016. Total cost of this program in 2016? $71 billion.

Where do those money come from? Middle class American who pay tax, who serve in military, who love their country, and who are called "deplorable" by Hillary! If $71 billion were spent on highway building, it would complete 214,000 miles of highway, and hire 2 million people! (According to Federal Highway Administration estimates) That impact was from a one-year spending.

Obama did not figure out why he failed in achieving "economic justice", despite of brutal robbery of middle class Americans, and stealing from future generations. Had those money being spend on right investments, GDP would have grown at 10%! Would have created millions jobs and a rebirth of middle class! Instead of growing the economy in a capitalistic way (the American way), he steered America to a dead-end welfare state that handout food stamps, free medical care, and free education (to half the America, paid by another half).

Consequence? Not only he did not reduce income gap, but also he flamed social hatred, anger and division.

After hand out food stamp so that people buy lots of beer and burger, and eat and party, what about heart disease, diabetes, and cancer that are sure to follow?

Give them Obama Care! What amazingly generous, caring, loving President! To his voters, he is only next to God. Actually, he is the God!

Obama robbed one group of Americans, and gave to another group. Is this a "progression" and "justice" of human society? Who give the President that power to do so? What is the next thing on his agenda? Confiscate all private properties and manage them by Fannie and Freddie? Pay every citizen equal stipend by the government and work as slave?

He loaded tax burdens on half of the population, and gave another half a free ride. That type of government is called "gang government" and, Obama was the gang head. All those stealing and robbery were a declared war on middle class Americans, in the name of progression, equality, and justice!

Calling him a communist or Marxist is probably a praise that he did not deserve. He has no ideological depth. He and his team are pitiful frogs in a well, which only see a small patch of sky. What he did not see, the bigger part of sky, is that the American President has to LEAD the world. Unfortunately, he led a mafia government that fought an economic war on good Americans - those hard working, tax paying, war fighting, "real" American (and majority of them happen to be Christians).

While Obama fought an economic civil war on middle class American, rest of the world are leap-frogging on economic growth, military strength, and technological advancement. During the 60s, the daily life of American, with car, TV, Rock-n-Roll was envied by the world; Today the world have caught up with our living standard, infrastructure, industrial prowess, and nearly every measurement.

In 2009, China also implemented a fiscal stimulus plan ($586 billion, or 4 trillion RMB) that is similar to Obama's in size, but China's plan resulted in far significant economic growth and job creation. Through the recession of 2008-2010, China sustained GDP growth at >12% annually. By 2016, China's GDP is equivalent to 59% of US GDP; While in 2008, China GDP is less than 30% of US. China doubled GDP during Obama time, America declined.

During those years, in Shanghai, China, a city with 20 million people, high-rise office buildings pop up like mushrooms. They were designed by European architect, structured with gigantic steel frame, shaped in futuristic fantasy, decorated by LED nights. There are no comparisons in the world!

A job well done, Mr. Obama!

"Those Jobs Aren't Coming Back" –Steve Jobs, Feb 2011

Obama campaigned on promises that he can create jobs and close income gaps for his voters, but he failed horrendously. He has no clue how to create jobs for the mass Americans. Like his Democrat elites, he was surrounded by tech CEOs and believed in the fantasy that Internet companies, such as Amazon, Google, and Facebook, would bring prosperity. He attended those tech and media conferences, and schmoozed with entrepreneurs, artists, and bankers.

Unfortunately, those Internet startups had the highest failure rate, and did not have much impact on job market. More often than not, improving efficiency means net job loss, not growth, such as the proliferating of Microsoft Office reduced jobs for secretaries.

Despite passing stimulus plans and added astronomic $9 trillion debt, US economy grew at less than 2% per year. Recovery was slow, and was sadly a jobless recovery. Inner city crime skyrocketed during his years. It is not hard to explain rising crimes - inner city youngsters without job are destined to sell drugs, commit crime, and even attack policemen. Those kids have no education, no job, and no future. Obama gave them food stamps, but not hopes.

Job loss continued in manufacturing. Despite of massive stimulus and modest recovery, 2 million manufacturing jobs are lost during Obama time. Manufacturing employed 14 million workers in 2008, counting for 11% of total non-farm employment. By 2016, total manufacturing employment has declined to 12 million, 10% of total employment. Many factories packed up for overseas, leaving no hopes for local workers. For example, at the peak of GM, the company hired 511,000 American workers in 1979, the year of peak manufacturing employment, at 19.5 million, in US history. Today GM employee: 54,000. When GM went bankrupt in 2009, hundreds of thousands workers were out of job. The only mitigation Obama did was to add those workers on federal long-term disability insurance. (part of 2009 stimulus plan)

It is so sad that Made in USA once was the symbol of pride and quality during WWII. The prowess of American industrial capabilities were once unparalleled in the world - M4 tanks of US army, the 2nd most produced tank for allied forces, were made by precision machines, while Soviet T-34 was jokingly made by hand (with appalling low quality). In 1985, while America produced 11 millions cars, and China manufactured 5,200 cars (imported 350,000 from overseas) that year. But, in 2014 alone, China produced 20 million passenger cars!

With no job available, teenage crimes skyrocketed, and racial tension flared over the years. Riots happened every time when a black person was shot by police at crime scenes. During 8 years, 162 mass shooting occurred, a record in history. (Average was 20 mass shooting during Clinton and Bush years)

- ✓ In July 2010, Oakland CA, riot erupted shortly after Obama being in office, caused massive looting, damaged properties, and trashed the city.
- ✓ In 2012, after suspected gang member, Manuel Diaz, ran from police and was shot to death, local crowds gathered and threw objects at police. The situation escalated shortly after, many rioters started fires, smashed windows and throwing rocks at officers.
- ✓ In March 2013, protest erupted in Brooklyn, New York, after 16-year-old Kimani Gray was shot. Furious protestants pitched bricks, bottles and garbage at police.
- ✓ Riot also happened after Freddie Gray's death, triggered a massive riot in Baltimore in April 2015.

Are police officers heartless, merciless racists who intentionally killed black victims? Maybe some policy overreacted in some situations, but majority police in America are no doubt professionals, who do their job with bravery, honesty and sound judgment. Many of police officers were killed at work by criminal thugs. Their sacrifice, bravery, and strength kept our society in peace and order.

In many cases of riot, Obama sided with the minority group, and infuriated police and American public. If President sided along racial line, how could people respect the law and the Presidency? How could Obama face the family members of police officers who died at work? When NYPD held funeral for fellow officer on Fifth Avenue, the anger of police did not erupt in shouting and screaming, but in their solemn silence on their stern face and expression. Nothing can change their unshakable faith in their country, in the people, and in America.

Frustrated by failure and inefficiency in creating jobs for America, and by eruption of racial tensions, Obama arranged many meetings with Silicon Valley big shots, including Steve Job at a Feb 2011 dinner. Tech is the shining beacon of US economy, and Obama's fantasy is to create more companies like Apple, Amazon and Google.

Apple hired 700,000 factory workers in China, and another 30,000 engineers to manage those workers. Additionally, contractors of Apple employed over 500,000 in its supply chains. When asked how to bring those Apple employments back to US, Jobs' reply was unambiguous, "Those jobs aren't coming back," he said.

"Companies once felt an obligation to support American workers, even when it wasn't the best financial. That's disappeared. Profits and efficiency have trumped generosity." said Betsey Stevenson, the chief economist at the Labor Department of Obama Administration. It sounded really pitiful for an economist to make that comment. Begging for business to create jobs in US was never effective. Business was never driven by sacrifice and generosity, but by profits and earnings.

What Obama did not understand (also incapable) is that tax and tariff sway business decisions. While it is hard to cut the salary of American workers to match Chinese standard, Obama can change tax code and tariff to put pressure on Apple. Apple made its decision of manufacturing sites on tax rate, tariff, business regulation, labor cost etc. If government had changed tariff, if Obama had cut corporate tax to make China site less profitable, Apple would have returned those positions to California overnight. No single word of begging was needed!

Globalization is the real cause of massive job loss and income gap. The collapse of Berlin Wall and Soviet Union in 1989 started the globalization that wrecked the American labor market. Through the 70s and 80s, there were some job losses due to competition, such as the US auto industry lost market share to Japanese car makers. And adoption of computer in work place improved productivity and reduce job opportunities for certain professionals. (Microsoft Office reduced the number of secretaries, Amazon closed many small book stores.), those job losses were reasonably absorbed by other sectors over time. For example, as the middle class enjoyed newly created wealth, they have more time for leisure traveling and entertainment, have accesses to newly invented medicines, and have a better life quality. Those sectors created new jobs that offset losses from traditional manufacturing and retailing.

The collapse of Berlin wall brought in sudden opening of global markets, and availability of massive, cheap labor force in Eastern Europe and in China. Corporations quickly figured out that given high labor cost and high tax rate in America, business will be much better off conducing manufacturing in overseas and selling in US, or find new suppliers in South America or China to reduce costs. At the end of the day, business is responsible for its shareholders. If maximizing shareholders value is the fiduciary duty of management team, sourcing to overseas is both morally and economically justified. Who would care those workers left behind in the dust belt of America?! It is their own duty to adapt and to find new jobs.

Society will absorb those labor force as before, economists murmured, even though their inner voice was saying the opposite. Corporations have no responsibilities for those expensive, not-so-productive American workers, CEOs said in private with no guilt. As the globalization gained momentums, more and more factories left America, from shoes and closes, to home appliance, to auto parts and machinery, and eventually computers, cell phones and semiconductors...

What is left in America? Shining, grand office buildings owned by banks and by rich hedge fund managers who work there, contrast sharply with massive unemployment and poverty in rusty, industrial belts of America, epitomized by Detroit.

Under WTO and NAFTA and many ridiculously unfair trade agreements, America border is wide open for foreign goods to flood. Why would US government sign those agreements that are detrimental and unfair to American "vital interest"? The truth is that politicians and many Congress are traitors! They are selling American public interests for the benefits of interest groups and their own pockets. Those shameless, guilty politician betrayed America, betrayed their soul! Obama was the head of all betrayals.

Despite astronomical trade deficit and job loss, Walmart, Target, CVS, and other big retailers, with more than half of their goods imported, were lobbying against border tax on foreign goods, which would raise prices of merchandises flooding from overseas. They claim that border tax would increase prices for US consumers!

What a falsely, misleading and shameless claim? Do US consumers prefer to be jobless and buy Nike shoes at $40 or to be fully employed and buy Nike shoes at $50?

Americans know the answer!

Large corporations' profits skyrocketed in past three decades, and profits margin hit all time high. In 1989, at the eve of globalization, S&P 500's net margin was at 4%, and the net margin reached 10% in 2016! As the stock market rebounded and wealth accumulation hit a new high, globalization won! America won!

Sadly, it is not that simple. Only the top 1% American won.

Globalization killed American middle class! Income distribution drastically shifted from a shape of potbelly to a pyramid. It all started with a gradual outsourcing, and then built few new plants, and finally thorough relocation of headquarters and tax domiciles to overseas.

Obama and Democrats orchestrated this globalization that benefited interest groups and his money "friends". For those Americans who lost jobs, Obama told them that they had to be better trained and better educated. He draw from his own life experience that poor kids can success if they do well in school, in college, they can climb to top of the world. Boy Obama was born in poverty, but he was smart, he studies hard and exceled in law school. Hence, America's economic problem is an education problem, and personal effort problem.

"And that is a dangerous and growing inequality and lack of upward mobility that has jeopardized middle-class America's basic bargain -- that if you work hard, you have a chance to get ahead. I believe this is the defining challenge of our time: Making sure our economy works for every working American. It's why I ran for President."

"It was at the center of last year's campaign. It drives everything I do in this office. Technology made it easier for companies to do more with less, eliminating certain job occupations. A more competitive world lets companies ship jobs anywhere. And as good manufacturing jobs automated or headed offshore, workers lost their leverage, jobs paid less and offered fewer benefits." Obama said on Dec 4th, 2013

Typical politicians' tactics! Blames something else when it is his fault. When millions lost their homes, Obama hand out candies. He misled American for eight yeas, and wasted trillions.

Is American really hopeless in creating jobs and bring back manufacture? NO, America can do manufacturing.

In Feb 2017, CNN reported that Apple is already secretly planning to move production plants back to California. "Apple asked both Foxconn and Pegatron, the two iPhone assemblers, in June to look into making iPhones in the U.S.," the Nikkei Asian Review reported, citing a source. It is also worthy note that this happened without implementing corporate tax cut and tariff hike. Once sound tax changes are in place, more productions will move back in downfall. Many SME, like insulin pump maker, Insulet, are already making the move.

Thank you, Mr. Steve Jobs. Those jobs are returning to America!

Failed President And His Failed Policies

When Obama started, job market was a mess. After 8 years, he made the situation worse.

Americans need job of all kinds. Technology and innovation can not solve the problem. Personal efforts and education cannot solve the problem. Obama's annual budget, robbed the middle class and gave to the poor, was a Robin Hood thinking, which has never, and will never, work to solve social inequality. Innovation is always good, however, innovations do not necessarily translate into job creations. Amazon killed mom-pop bookstores, Microsoft Office replaced secretary jobs, and Uber drives taxi drivers out of work. While those firms simultaneous created new employments, net effects are often job loss, because of improved efficiency.

During the Obama Presidency, unemployment rate fell, but not that meaningful. The real job situation was still depressingly bad. In rusty belt communities, thousands and thousands people have left job market for years and "no hope" to find any. Those people knew what is really happening, not the labor department statisticians. Although the official unemployment has declined to 6%, labor participation rate has declined by 5% in last decade. Many people took early retirement or part time jobs. If add back those under-employed, unemployment rate at the end of 2016 is still around 10%.

Obama never paid serious attentions to blue collar jobs, as he believed, Americans should move up on the ladder of global job market, and be retrained, retooled to for jobs at the new economy, the dazzling high tech and internet companies. Those manufacturing jobs are gone forever, and will not return. This is very much a consensus of Democrats since Clinton time. In a fiction *"Primary Color"* written by Joe Klein, the Presidential candidate, Jack Stanton (which almost exactly mimic Bill Clinton) told a shipyard audience during his campaign that:

"So let me tell you this: No politician can bring these shipyard jobs back. Or make your union strong again. No politician can make it be the way it used to be. Because we're living in a new world now, a world without borders -- economically, that is. Guy can push a button in New York and move a billion dollars to Tokyo before you blink an eye. We've got a world market now. And that's good for some. In the end, you've gotta believe it's good for America. We come from everywhere in the world, so we're gonna have a leg up selling to everywhere in the world. Makes sense, right? But muscle jobs are gonna go where muscle labor is cheap -- and that's not here. So if you want to compete and do better, you're gonna have to exercise a different set of muscles, the ones between your ears. And anyone who gets up here and says he can do it for you isn't leveling with you. So I'm not gonna insult you by doing that. I'm going to tell you this: This whole country is gonna have to go back to school. We're gonna have to get smarter, learn new skills. And I will work overtime figuring out ways to help you get the skills you need. I'll make you this deal: I will work for you. I'll wake up every morning thinking about you. I'll fight and worry and sweat and bleed to get the money to make education a lifetime thing in this country, to give you the support you need to move on up."

Obama embraced new economy fantasy like the rest of Democrat, talked empty about innovation and tech to replace old economy, spend big money on clean energy and high tech gimmicks that wasted billions and never paid off. Obama attended Annual South by SouthWest each year, the annual tech, media and startup gather in Austin, TX. He said in early 2016, "I'll travel to Austin, Texas, to visit South by Southwest. It's an annual gathering of some of our most creative thinkers, coders, makers, and entrepreneurs from across the country. And while I'm there, I'm going to ask everyone for ideas and technologies that can help update our government and our democracy to be as modern and dynamic as America itself."

His obsession with Internet startups and entrepreneurs generated nothing other than publicity and image of being a tech geek. He surrounded himself with tech CEOs, and academic over-achievers. Obama's cabinet looked like a reunion of his friends and teachers from Harvard, plus Noble laureates to proved his "progressive" and "inclusive". Even foreign reporters noticed that *sel*dom has any foreign country been run so completely by such as narrowly defined elites.

His cabinet members, made of elite individuals representing various interest groups, are totally out touch with the main street. No surprise, his policy and judgment about America are entirely off track. Elite cabinet and law school friends were no guarantee for economic growth. Frustrated by his failures, Obama blamed American worker of their lousy education, lack of social justice, not hard working enough. While rushing to overseas continued and exacerbated, Obama shrugged. Sorry, Obama cannot help those poorly educated "deplorable". They have to re-educate themselves, compete harder on global markets, to climb on social ladder, like Obama did.

Education cannot solve economic problem alone. A few super smart, like Obama, may get a job at White House, or start an Internet company. Those startups may hire a dozen people, or even hundreds people, but they could not replace the millions jobs that have been lost to overseas. In small towns and inner cities, Americans need jobs in millions.

Obama and Democrats team, stayed on the course of WTO, NAFTA, TPP and so on, left American border wide opened to foreign goods and illegal immigrants. Let foreign firms exploit US market, stole technology, bought US factory and machinery at yard sale price, and returned with high value added goods - toys, clothes, shoes, electronics, computers, drones... while did nothing to protect factory workers, veterans and small town Americans. How could that situation help "close economic gap" and reward Obama's voters? Americans are losing altogether, regardless race, origin, gender and religion.

During those years, Obama thoroughly and entirely abandoned America heritage and value. Because in his root, he is not part of America heritage. Born to rebellious, hipster, atheist mother and Muslim father in Hawaii, he grew up in Indonesia. His college time in California was a "good time". His baptism by Reverend Jeremiah Wright brought him to a home that preached racial hatred and anti-white heresy. He does not share, does not connect, and does not belong to American values.

"We read about Ann in her son's autobiography... refusing to accompany her Indonesian husband to dinner parties with visiting American businessmen. There were her own people, Ann's husband would remind her; at which, the son tells us, 'my mother's voice rise to almost a shout. They are not my people.'" Ann Dunham's son is Barack Hussein Obama. (*Suicide of a Superpower*, Patrick Buchanan)

During his visit to Turkey, April 2009, Obama remarked, *"I've said before that one of the great strengths of the United States is – although as I mentioned we have a very large Christian population – we do not consider ourselves a Christian nation, or a Jewish nation or a Muslim nation. We consider ourselves a nation of citizens who are bound by ideals and a set of values."*

What are the "set of values" of Obama?

Obama's ideals are total breakaways from traditional American values. He is an international hipster; and had no association with Christian value, which is foundational and fabric of American society. He is a fake Christian and takes no pride in America heritage. During his youth, he smoked pot and had a good time in college. Hedonism and drugs were his religion.

After moving to White House, written on his face are self-satisfaction and narcissism. He is so proud of ruling over white people as a black President. To him and Michele, their mission was to lead a war of black over white, to enrich the black and rob the white, not to lead America to its greatness in the world. His eloquent speeches of reducing economic injustice, and creating opportunities for everyone are entirely fake and empty (He did a great of job impoverishing the white though)

During eight years, He was busy helping the black for "fair shot" to achieve "economic justice", while denied fair shots for the white and other ethnic groups. He was the preeminent, ultimate racist in American history!

For many who consider Obama being the victory of America's progressive movement, and winner of the final trophy – running White House, what has he done for America?

-Friends and foes lost respects to America in many aspects on global affairs
-Lost competition in countless manufacturing capacities and military prowess
-Enemy became stronger and bolder, and challenged America on every front.

Facing the killing of policemen, riots in cities, and the black's suffering of poverty, his judgments were wrong, his views were biased, and his solutions were total failures.

Obama felt no guilty of accumulating $9 trillion dollars debt on American people. If America went bankrupt today, with the money he rewarded his "friends" and stole from Treasury, he and Michele can live like a king in Kenya or Indonesia, where his parents belonged. They cannot care less about America, as Michele said she is not "proud of America".

Form Clinton to Obama, Democrats has alienated labor union and American workers, while entirely embraced with Wall Street, hedge fund managers, internet entrepreneurs, coastal well-educated elites, and non-white immigrants. During Obama time, Democrat thoroughly ended being blue collar's party.

Obama failed his Presidency. He failed American who voted him to the White House. He delivered nothing other than $9 trillion debt, loss of American power, food stamps, expansion of federal agencies, and an over-promised, expensive Obama care.

And more importantly, he destroyed Christian and American values.

Christian Value And Women's March

Shortly after the inauguration of President Trump, millions women marched in Washington DC and other major cities in US on Jan 21st, 2017. The crowd did not have a specific goal to protest, was vaguely against Trump's victory, with a goal of safeguarding women's rights, immigration, environment, LGBT, etc.

This march was shockingly wrong directed. They should have marched 8 years ago, because Obama has been destroying Christian value, degraded women's status, and welcomed immigrants whose religion deeply belittles women and advocates polygamous. Where were those women by then?

Trump is not an enemy of women's rights and equality and he fought hard to bring back prosperity to America. For many years, America is on a wrong track that lead to slip and slump on the world order. Each citizen, women and men of America, should celebrate and support a President who promised to fight against the betrayal, injustice and pessimism.

It is the moment in history that people, each and everyone of American, take back the government from Washington's establishments, who have not passed single policy to protect American workers and American jobs, and who have left American border wide open to criminals and terrorists.

For those who marched on that day, please remember Elizabeth Warren said at the rally, "We will not build that stupid wall."

Illegal immigrants have flooded American cities and towns, with drugs, guns, outlaws and criminals. With wrong foot starting in

America, those illegals are destined for drug trafficking and gang crimes. If immigration law can be broken, what other law that can be broken? If laws are not obeyed by citizens, America will end in chaos and turmoil. Is that what Americans want? Is that what Elizabeth Warren want?

Illegal immigrants in America are like cancer in human body. Either cut out the cancer so that body can survive, or the cancer will take over and kills the body. There is nothing between to choose from.

Why did those Democrats against the border wall, which seems a so-obvious, low-IQ, absolutely necessary measure? The answer is that they are selling conscious and soul to buy votes from those illegal immigrants. After legalized those illegal people, and gave them food stamps, free medicine and free education, Democrats forever own their votes and supports, while free goodies are being paid by other half, "real" Americans. Democrats are betraying real Americans!

Those politicians enriched themselves at the expense of American's future (piling up national debt is a crime committed by Obama and Congress). The accumulated national debt is deeply shameful and scary. Can our children and grand children ever pay back those debts? Whose interest is the Congress representing?

For those marched at the protest and refuse to accept Trump as the new President, think for a moment: Trump said extremely loudly and clearly that his agenda are to make "America First". "Politicians prospered – but the jobs left, and the factories closed. The establishment protected itself, but not the citizens of our country" as Trump said at the inauguration. He will implement polices to bring job back to America, and "Buy American and Hire American"

To American women, anything wrong with those goals? Do American women prefer to be jobless, and lose competition to foreign countries? Do women prefer America to slide and slump into a 2nd world? Do women prefer to legalize polygamy in America?

In last eight years, our enemies are growing stronger and bolder. With a weak and coward President in white house, enemies are bullying America military and threatening American interests! If American people continue waste time squabbling on social nonsense like "black life matters", "toilet right", and "political correctness", American is losing on global competitions. If you are a loser, no wonder you are feeling "lack of hope".

While American population is become very diverse, the core value of our nation is being forgotten. Those core value, founded on Christianity, brought us together from all over the world and is the fabric of our society. We can NOT abandon Christian values and our believing.

In 1915, Ted Roosevelt addressed about ethnical loyalty to America, "The one absolutely certain way of bringing this nation to ruin, of preventing all possibility of its continuing to be a nation at all, would be to permit it to become a tangle of squabbling nationalities, an intricate knot of German-Americans, Irish-Americans, English-Americans, French-Americans, Scandinavian-Americans or Italian-Americans, each preserving its separate nationality, each at heart feeling more sympathy with Europeans of that nationality, than with the other citizens of the American Republic ... There is no such thing as a hyphenated

American who is a good American. The only man who is a good American is the man who is an American and nothing else."

Trump, and conservatives, is NOT the enemy of women or equality. The focus about a President is what he stands for, and what he fights to achieve. Trump stand for majority of Americans, who lost job and were left behind, who paid tax, fought in the army, who insist on Christian values and integrity, who worked hard and built American glories.

Obama stood for the black and fought a war on the white. During his administration, he handed out food stamps, social welfares, and free medical cares to those who voted for him. And he stole billions from general budget to fund NGOs that are run by his "friends".
What has Obama achieved? Despair among black population, loss of jobs in million, rise of crime, decline of real income, loss of military superiority. Those who lost jobs knew what really situation is. And those people elected Trump!

Did black benefit from a black President? Not much, they are worse off than 8 years ago! Despite Obama handed them welfare checks and job quotas, total job market sunk, and drag down all boats. Although stock and house market rebounded, real income for majority of the population declined.

Without job, without future, many young black kids are selling drugs for living. If they had decent job and promising future, they would not be criminal! But, the reality is "those jobs are gone". Despite favors from "their" President, they suffered economically and socially, along with rest of the country.

Americans, if you share the feeling of "lack of hope" with Michele, blame Obama!

Our Infrastructure Is Deplorable! - Build Highways, Build Airports And Build The Border Wall!

In Sep 1959, when the former USSR leader, Nikita Khrushchev, toured US, he was so impressed by the interstate highway that connected America, and felt very jealous of what America has achieved since WWII, and American daily life. Upon his visit to China, he told Chairman Mao that America was so rich and prosperous. After brief silence, Mao, resenting Khrushchev's betrayal of Stalin and insisting on creed of communism, sniffed and said, "is that all you can see? Can not you tell their capitalism is near collapsing?"

Of course, this was a telltale. Nevertheless, the interstate highway system was "the greatest public-works program in the history of the world." (Sinclair Weeks, Secretary of Commerce). With 41,000 miles limited access toll road, the system connect America from west to east, and north to south, big cities and small towns; Indeed, 90% of cities with populations of >50,000 are on the network.

The system was envisioned in 30s by FDR to pull the nation out of Great Depression. Nevertheless, WWII interrupted the plan to build a national super highway. While regional highway and metropolitan throughway were build during 30s and 40s, the most important milestone was the *Federal-Aid Highway Act of 1956*, signed by President Eisenhower in June 1956, bringing the connectivity and convenience to a new level never achieved before.

What is particular amazing is that, despite total budget of the project of $35 billion, the funding will come from toll and gasoline tax, not on federal debt. Federal government distributed

$25 billion among the states over the 13 years to cover 90% of the cost, with rest being funded by states.

Today, that many parts of that system are worn out by traffic and weather, and lack of maintenance. 1/3 of existing major roads are ranked "in poor or mediocre condition" by the American Society of Civil Engineers. As famously stated by former Vice President Biden, in regard to LaGuardia airport, "we have a third world infrastructure, and we are sick of it" Because cash flow from gasoline tax is in decline, the money barely covers maintenance with a very little for new construction. As for the spending on road as percentage of GDP, USA ranks 9th in the world.

In May 2013, the Skagit River bridge on I5 (in Washington State) collapsed. The bridge was completed in 1955. In Aug 2007, the Mississippi River bridge on I35, (in Minnesota), collapsed. Other than those well-publicized collapses, road condition, such as I95, is notoriously bad with potholes and cracks.

Since the completion of interstate highway decades ago, construction of new highway slowed to trickles. Economic growth on coastal cities has spurred traffic growth beyond the capacity of existing roads. From example, from 1989 to 2010, traffic on highways increased by 39%. But, total mileage of highway rose by only 4%.

Why did not we have money to build airport and road? Where did the government spending go? Well, Obama spend the $787 billion on a stimulus package, only $27.5 billion was spend on construction.

What if $100 billion had been spending on road and airport? Or even 400 billion?

Road building create jobs with multiplier effects: not only those direct job involved in construction, but also indirect job in manufacturing of construction materials, such as steel frames, cement. Additionally, the project can induce news jobs when worker spend their earning on food, housing, medical care etc. Hence, 1 direct job created in construction can cascade into 2-3 jobs in total.

To what degree can infrastructure spending creates jobs? The Federal Highway Administration estimated that with $1 billion spending on roads, it would create 9,500 direct construction jobs, 4,300 indirect jobs, and 14,000 induced jobs. A total of 27,800 job!

If Obama had spent $100 billion out of the stimulus plan on construction, it would have created 2.8 million jobs in 2009! (At the peak of the financial crisis, unemployed hit 25 million people)

If $400 billion on construction, job creation would be 11 million! (total employment in manufacturing is 11 million today) The nation would have been in shortage of labor! And out of recession immediately!

The failure of Obama Presidency can not be over-stated, and can not be forgiven.

Chapter 8 – Find Real Truth of Climate Change

"Proponents of cuts in greenhouse gases cited the (ice cap) meltdown as proof that human activities are propelling a slide toward climate calamity."-New York Times

"Spring comes earlier than it used to in Tasiilaq, Greenland. The snow starts to melt weeks before it did even a decade ago in this small Inuit settlement, while ice that was once a permanent fixture on the nearby slopes now sloughs off during the short summer."-Financial Times

"1998 summer was the hottest summer of millennium" -American Geophysical Union news release.

"The polar ice cap as a whole is shrinking. Images from NASA satellites show that the area of permanent ice cover is contracting at a rate of 9 percent each decade. If this trend continues, summers in the Arctic could become ice-free by the end of the century" -NASA

"Early-Blooming Wildflowers: A Sign of Global Warming?" – Time

Are We Heating Up The Earth

Every single day, global warming is the headline on newspapers. We heard millions of times that earth temperature keeps on rising; if not curtailed, anthropogenic global warming will flood and world and destroy humanity. Environmentalism is the new global religion preached in every corner of the world.

James Hansen is the godfather of global warming who has rung the bell of CO_2 warning since the 80s. He joined NASA in 1967 and was the pioneer of building a model to systematically measure and monitor global surface temperature. In 1981, his publication in *Science* was the first to demonstrate rising global temperature in the past century, to predict earth warming (from a cooling between 1940-1970) and increased influence of anthropogenic CO_2.

Hansen and his team further analyzed data of surface air temperature from 1880 to 1985. The result was published in 1987. They concluded that warming in the past century was found to be 0.5-0.7 °C, with warming similarly in both hemispheres. And they also analyzed the correlation of temperature data from stations in different distances.

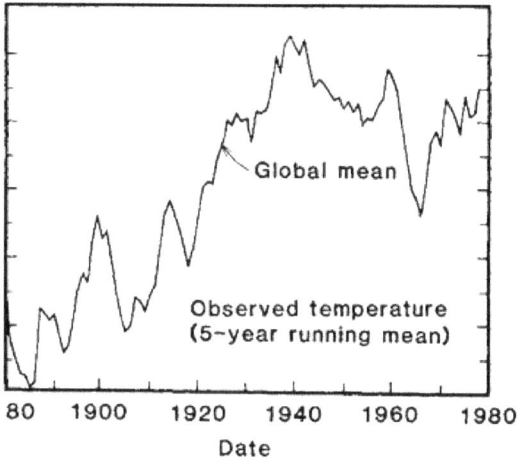

Source: Hansen etc. Climate impact of increasing atmospheric carbon dioxide. *Science*, **213**, 957-966.

He updated this research in 1999 to report that 1998 was the warmest year since the instrumental data began in 1880. They also found that the rate of temperature change was larger than any time in instrument history. Hansen stated in an interview in January 2009, "We cannot now afford to put off change any longer. We have to get on a new path within this new administration. We have only four years left for Obama to set an example to the rest of the world. America must take the lead."

The conclusion that 1998 summer was the hottest was also supported by research work from Michael Mann, who conducted a tree-ring based study of earth temperature to finish his Ph.D. at University of Massachusetts. Mann's study was a post child of researches that proved global warming in last millennium, was cited and quoted by many global warming publications.

In his publication, Mann said: "the 1990s was the warmest decade, and 1998 the warmest years, at moderately high levels of confidence." In last 1000 years, temperature has been very stable until the start of industrialization, based on his study.

The work done by Michael Mann at University of Massachusetts, Phil Jones and Keith Briffa *of* Climatic Research Unit (CRU) at the University of East Anglia (UK) are the basis for IPCC's conclusion that "the rate and magnitude of global or hemispheric surface 20th century warming is likely to have been the largest of the millennium, with the 1990s and 1998 likely to have been the warmest decade and year"

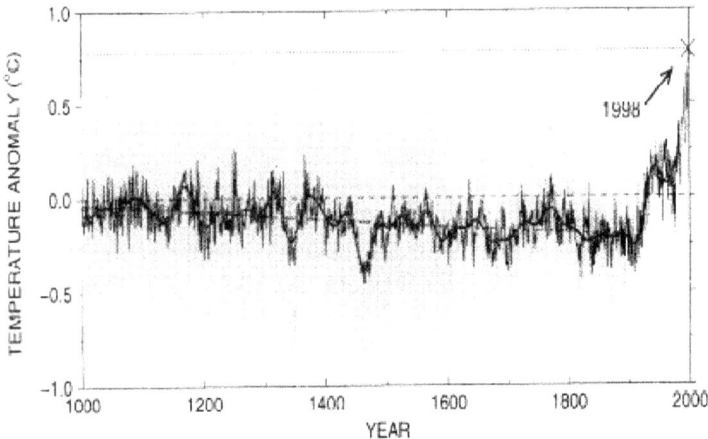

Source: "Northern Hemisphere temperatures during the past millennium: inferences, uncertainties, and limitations" by Michael e. Mann. Geophysical research letters, VOL 26, No. 6, Pages 759-762, March 15, 1999.

In 2001, this "hockey stick" shaped graph of global temperature was incorporated in IPCC's *Third Assessment Report,* as a decisively convincing evidence of global warming since Industrial Revolution.

Based on those studies, IPCC and Al Gore believed that "science is settled". The Earth's temperature has been rising since the industrial revolution, and this rise was mainly contributed by burning coal and oil fossil fuels. CO_2 emission, as a greenhouse gas, was pointed as the culprit for causing rising earth temperature. The rise of CO_2 concentration in atmosphere was believed to be anthropogenic and causing global warming.

FLAWS OF THOSE STUDIES:

Counter argument 1:
Mann's study was challenged by a Canadian statistician, Stephen McIntyre, who was a mining industry expert. In 2002, McIntyre immediate cast suspicion on Mann's data analysis. He had extensive experience in rejecting estimates of mineral reserves made by their owners. He ran a Climate Audit blog, which questioned the validity of the statistical analyses used to create the 'hockey stick' graph. He also criticized the quality of global temperature data from NASA's Goddard Institute of Space Studies (GISS), headed by James Hansen.

By his relentless criticism and adamant request for data, methods and source codes from Mann, Mann reluctantly shared some of his data with McIntyre and then stopped. Eventually, Mann shared all the data after the intervention of National Science Foundation and Congressman Joe Barton. McIntyre conducted his own analysis of Mann's research data, using a different statistical method.

In 2003, Stephen McIntyre and Ross McKitrick published in the journal *Energy and Environment* 14(6) 751-772 "Corrections to the Mann *et al*. (1998) Proxy Data Base and Northern Hemisphere Average Temperature Series". In this publication,

McIntyre and McKitrick expressed their difficulty to reproduce the results of Mann.

The controversy of Mann's and other's research data attracted the attention of US Energy and Commerce Committee, which convened a team of scientists by the National Research Council to assess Mann's data. Additionally, Congressman Joe Barton requested Dr. Edward Wegman and another two statisticians to conduct the same analysis.

In 2006, the Wegman committee issued their reports that rejected the Mann's hockey stick graph, and supported McIntyre's conclusion. "In general, we found MBH98 and MBH99 to be somewhat obscure and incomplete and the criticisms of MM03/05a/05b to be valid and compelling" (Page 3 of Wegman report).

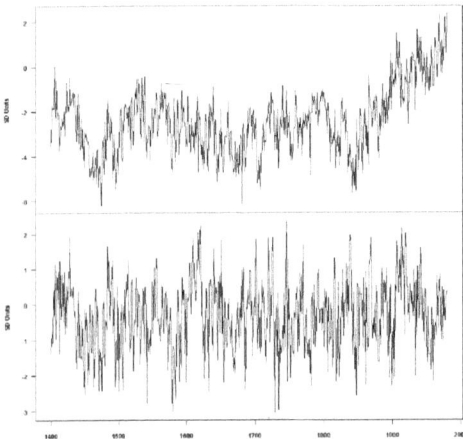

Source: Wegman report. Top panel is the Mann's original analysis and result. Bottom panel is the result based on a Wegman review that utilized a statistical method advocated by McIntyre.

In 2007, when IPCC published its *SUMMARY FOR POLICYMAKER* of its voluminous *Fourth Assessment Report* (AR-4), Mann's "hockey stick" graph was dropped.

Counter argument 2:
In 2001, Dr. Syun-Ichi Akasofu demonstrated that since 1660, central England has been gradually heating up at a rate of 0.5 Celsius degree per 100 years. However, this rising temperature is due to reversing from a little ice age, and the increase is linear and gradual. Industrialization in Europe, the United States and Japan did not cause any sudden acceleration of temperature rise. Dr. Syun-Ichi Akasofu, a Founding Director and Professor of Physics, Emeritus, was the director of the International Arctic Research Center of the University of Alaska. From the establishment of the research center in 1998 till January of 2007, Dr. Akasofu has published more than 550 professional journal articles, authored and co-authored 10 books, and has been invited to author many encyclopedia articles. His paper on the aurora published in 1964 was cited as one of the most quoted papers. His view was that much of the warming of the 20th century was a continuation of whatever natural trend that drove the increase in the previous century. That linear increase of 0.5 degree per 100 years, is likely to be a natural change, due to recovering from the little ice age.

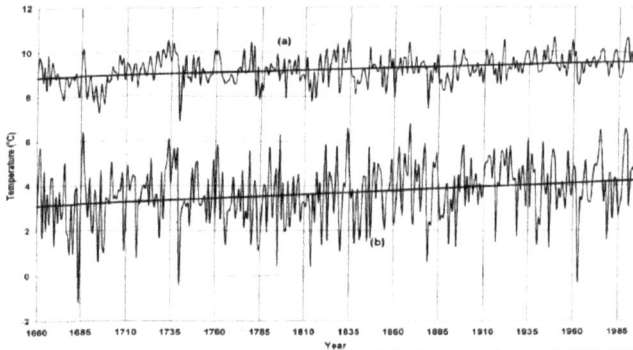

Figure 4: The linear trends for the temperature of central England over the period 1660-1996 for (a) the annual data, and (b) the winter months (December to February), show a marked warming. In both cases, this warming is significant, but although the temperature rise is greater in winter, this trend is less significant because the variance from year to year is correspondingly greater (Burroughs, 2001).

Source: Akasofu, University of Alaska.

Hence, the man-made greenhouse effect should be the difference between the actual rise of temperature and the natural trend. Nevertheless, the difference is so minuscule that no one would even call it global warming. CO_2 can cause greenhouse effects, but CO_2 alone cannot be the primary cause of global warming.

Counter argument 3:

In 2004, Polyakov etc published the average temperature record at the stations along the coast of the Arctic Ocean. We can see that the temperature rose rapidly between 1920 and 1940, and also from 1970 to 2000. What is striking is the drop in temperature from 1940 to 1960 in the Arctic, and the rise of CO_2 level from 290 ppm to 315 ppm. (according to Scripps Institution of Oceanography)

216

Source: Polyakov etc 2004. The red line is the rise of global temperature as reported in IPCC 2007 report. Arctic temperature rises more rapidly than the average temperature.

Correctly Measure Earth Surface Temperature

It is extremely difficult to measure a global average temperature because we can not install a thermometer on every inch of the earth. Temperature is measured at selected spots of the earth. Are those spots evenly distributed? No. Are there any biases of their locations? YES. Most land based weather station, built in the 1950s and 1960s, are located in the suburban areas of major cities because there was no need or necessity to know the temperature and weather in remote areas.

What happened in those suburban areas in the last decades? They are becoming urban areas! They are now surrounded by high-rises, by new power plants, by shopping malls and by cars driving through.

What are the effects of urban development on global reported temperature? Here is an example of weather stations located at different neighborhoods that have generated different trends of local climate trend. A measuring station in an undeveloped suburban neighborhood showed a cooling pattern, while a station on a residential area showed an upward trend of local temperature

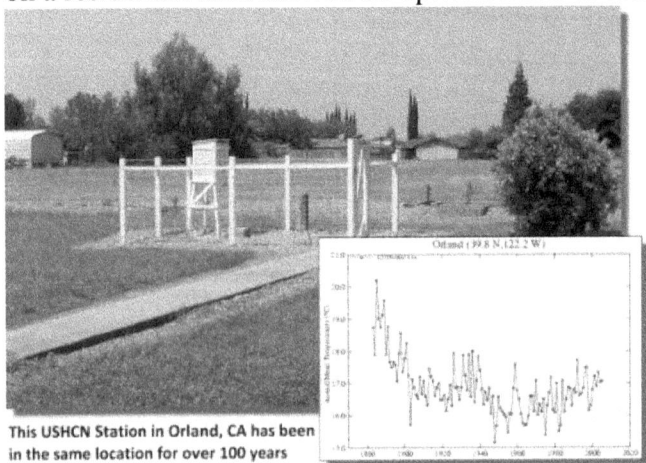

This USHCN Station in Orland, CA has been in the same location for over 100 years

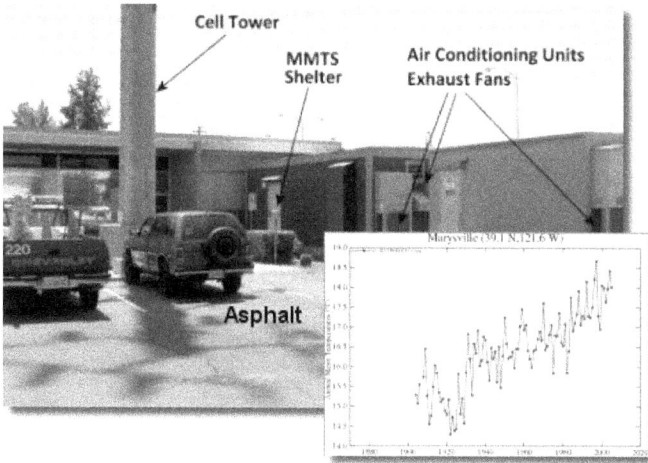

Source: USHCN

Dr. Ross McKitrick is a professor of environmental economics at University of Guelph, Canada. He is widely-cited in Canada and around the world as an expert on global warming and environmental policy issues. He has been interviewed by *Time*, *The New York Times*, *The Wall Street Journal*, *The National Post*, *The Globe and Mail*, the CBC, BBC, Bloomberg, Global TV, CTV, and several others.

He constructed this chart of overlapping average temperature and the number of global stations. There was a significant loss of stations since 1990 in the former Soviet Union, China, Africa and South America. This loss of stations coincided with a sudden rise of average temperature. Is it because those lost stations are in remote areas so that the remaining stations are mostly located near cities? We know that cities are heat islands.

A map of global weather stations shows clearly that they are distributed unevenly.

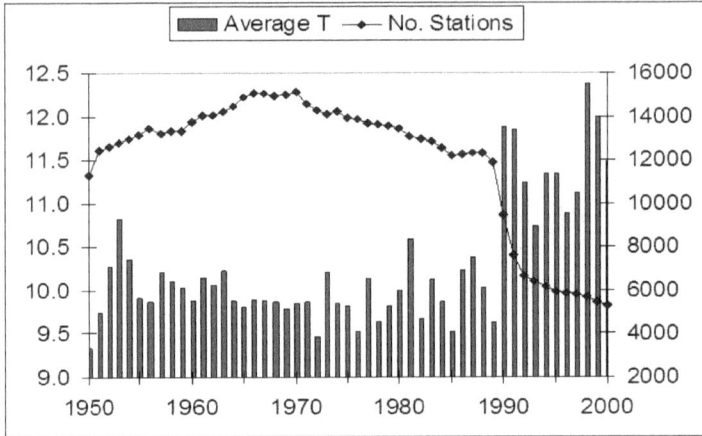

Source: Dr. Ross Mckitrick.
http://www.uoguelph.ca/~rmckitri/research/nvst.html

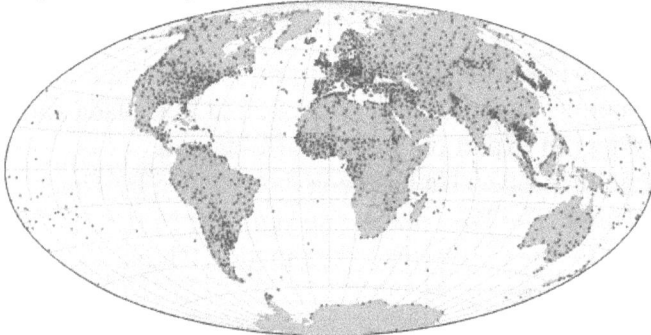

Source: NASA map by Robert Simmon, based on data from the National Climatic Data Center.

The bias from surface measurement of earth temperature is easy to understand. Hence, average of data from weather stations is not a reliable source to definitely answer the question of whether the earth is heating up or not. Sampling errors and surface variability can easy distort the conclusion. We have to find different ways to measure the earth temperature.

Can we measure the earth temperature of the air and of the ocean water? Yes, actually. We have the temperature data of the low atmosphere (called troposphere) from balloon carried instruments since 1958, and from satellite instruments since 1979. Those measurements should reflect the true earth surface temperature. According to IPCC advocated climate model, atmosphere temperature should rise if the earth surface warms up, because more radiation from the surface will heat up molecules in the air. The data came out from balloons and satellites disappointed believers of global warming. Those data did NOT show the same warming trend of earth temperature as was hoped. A report by the National Research Council in the late 1990s that reviewed the upper air temperature trends stated that:

"Data collected by satellites and balloon-borne instruments since 1979 indicate little if any warming of the low- to mid- troposphere—the atmospheric layer extending up to about 5 miles from the Earth's surface. Climate models generally predict that temperatures should increase in the upper air as well as at the surface if increased concentrations of greenhouse gases are causing the warming."

Not surprisingly, the significant discrepancy between weather station data and satellite data created huge controversies. US Climate Science Program took on the task of re-analyzing the data. After extensive efforts of different scientific bodies, they could still not agree on one definite conclusion. IPCC (of course) said that significant discrepancy no longer exists because errors in the satellite and radiosonde data have been identified and corrected. Others said that issues with reconciling data and models remain. Here is the chart from IPCC's report on this satellite issue. Honestly, there is no clear trend.

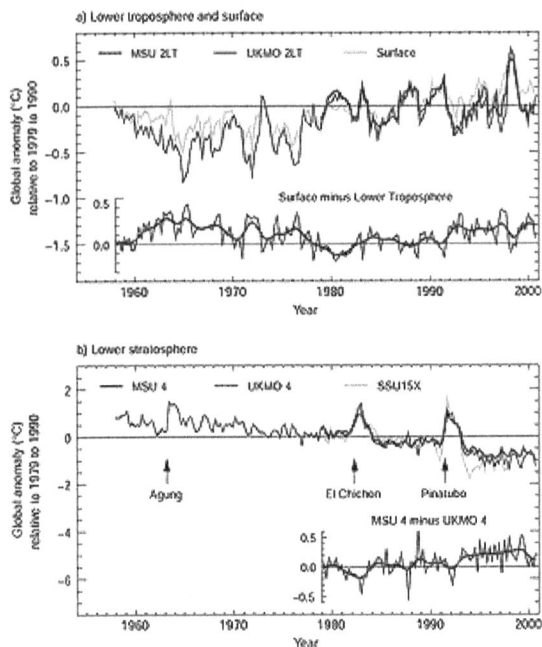

Source: IPCC - Climate Change 2001: Working Group I: The
Scientific Basis Figure 2.12

Does Anyone See More Hurricanes?

"Experts warn global warming likely to continue spurring more outbreaks of intense activity." — *Kevin Trenberth*
"Stronger Link Found between Hurricanes and Global Warming. A century's worth of records suggests that hurricanes are on the rise and a warming Atlantic is to blame." - David Biello

In the eyes of global warming, many naturally occurring events are the victim of rising earth temperature, including hurricane, flu, and even pest outbreak. Many publications, from scientific journals to newspapers, linked hurricanes to global warming. The 2005 Hurricane Katrina became such an easy scare tool to use. Due to lack of evidence and data, many of those articles drew their conclusions from suggestions and speculations.

Not only did they create media hypes, but also ridiculous jokes. Dr. Kevin Trenberth is a well-accomplished scientist as the Head of the Climate Analysis Section at the National Center for Atmospheric Research. He has published 450 scientific papers, including 47 books and 198 journal articles, which places him among the top 20 authors with highest citations in all of geophysics. He shared the 2007 Nobel Peace Price with Al Gore. In an article published in the *Scientific American*, June 17, 2007, "Warmer Oceans, Stronger Hurricanes. Evidence is mounting that global warming enhances a cyclone's damaging winds and flooding rains", he said that "The summer of 2004 seemed like a major wake-up call: an unprecedented four hurricanes hit Florida, and 10 typhoons made landfall in Japan—four more than the previous record in that region."

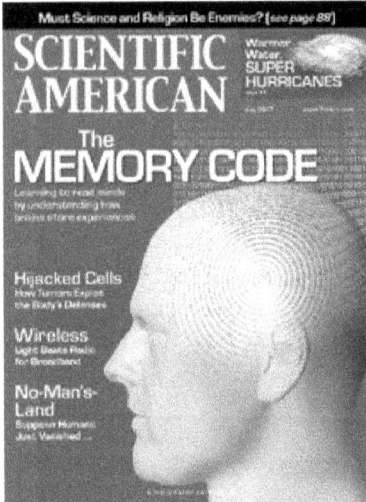

"Global climate change, and global warming in particular, create a different background environment in which the hurricanes are working," he said, "The sea surface temperatures are a little warmer, the whole environment is a bit wetter, there's more humidity, and that's the main fuel for hurricanes."

This sounded quite convincing and reasonable. However, there was no hard data from the past hurricane activities to support the conclusion. In 2005, while Dr. Trenberth was leading the effort to draft the *Fourth Assessment Report* of IPCC (AR-4 report) on hurricane activities, among the team scientists who were recruited to write for the report was the National Hurricane Center's chief scientist, Dr. Chris Landsea. It is a privilege to be a writer for this report as IPCC is the leading global organization focusing on climate issues. Dr. Landsea received the American Meteorological Society's Banner I. Miller award for the "best contribution to the science of hurricane and tropical weather forecasting."

While preparing for the write-up of the report, Dr. Landsea experienced a politicalized, non-objective process in citing evidences and drawing conclusions about hurricane and global warming. His concern about mis-representation of scientific data was dismissed by Dr. Trenberth and the rest of IPCC leadership.

In an open letter, Dr. Landsea wrote: "All previous and current research in the area of hurricane variability has shown no reliable, long-term trend up in the frequency or intensity of tropical cyclones, either in the Atlantic or any other basin."

"I personally cannot in good faith continue to contribute to a process that I view as both being motivated by pre-conceived agendas and being scientifically unsound. As the IPCC leadership has seen no wrong in Dr. Trenberth's actions and have retained him as a Lead Author for the AR4, I have decided to no longer participate in the IPCC AR4."

Fortunately, there are great scientists in the world who are objective, non-biased and insistent on their research. They enlighten humans understanding of nature, and help make right policies for the society and future generations. We owe them the biggest thanks.

Here are the data that demonstrated no increased frequency of storms and hurricane in last 50 years by Dr. Klotzbach.

Table 13: U.S. landfalling tropical cyclones by intensity during two 50-year periods.

YEARS	Named Storms	Hurricanes	Intense Hurricanes (Cat 3-4-5)	Global Temperature Increase
1900-1949 (50 years)	189	101	39	+0.4°C
1958-2007 (50 years)	165	82	33	

Source: Philip Klotzbach etc. 2007. Dept. of Atmospheric
Sciences, Colorado State University.

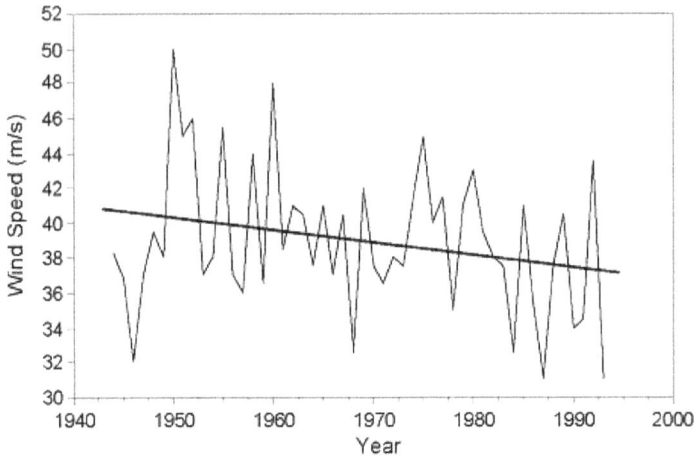

Source: Annual average maximum wind speeds recorded in
Atlantic basin tropical cyclones (Landsea C.W., et al., 1996).

**During the 2010 season, there was no hurricane landfall in US,
despite that 12 hurricanes formed in the Atlantic Ocean.** Now,
who and what should we believe about hurricanes and global
warming? And about CO_2 and climate change? Analyzing the
huge amount of climate data is not everyone's job. It needs
tremendous resources and efforts. Only the large scientific and
political bodies like IPCC or US Global Change Research
Program have the funding and scientists to conduct large scale
research and review. The rest of us can only read newspapers and
listen to the evening TV talks. It is very scary if those researches
are biased and politically motivated.

Who will safeguard the objectivity of our climate research?
Climate is constantly changing and is affected by many factors,
both earthly ones and extraterrestrial factors. Temperature will
move upward and downward, depending where we are in the

cycle. Change is constant. Supporting this view is British scientist Jane Francis, who maintains that: "What we are seeing really is just another interglacial phase within our big icehouse climate." Dismissing political calls for a global effort to reverse climate change, she said, "It's really farcical because the climate has been changing constantly... What we should do is be more aware of the fact that it is changing and that we should be ready to adapt to the change."

Al Gore: "Science is settled." Really? Is the earth temperature
higher than 100 year ago? 1,000 years ago? or 1 million years ago?

Earth temperature is NOT as what most believed stable year over
year. The earth has seasonal fluctuations. However, each year
when the earth returns to the same positions relative to the sun,
temperature is quite constant as it was. Astronomy studies told us
that sun and earth are both at relative stable mid-age, and fusion
reaction inside the sun will last another billions of years, keeping
the earth warm and constant.

Nevertheless, if we observe long-term trend of earth temperature,
we can immediately find that surface temperate has a cycle of
100,000 years. This phenomenon was discovered by Serbian civil
engineer and mathematician, Milutin Milankovic (1879-1958). In
last 800,000 years, Earth temperate fluctuated with a distinct
glacial and interglacial phase at an interval of about 100,000
years. In each 100,000 years, earth temperature also fluctuated in
shorter cycles, such as 40,000 year cycle, 21,000 cycle, 11 year
solar cycle. We can saw those cycles from tree rings and coral
patterns.

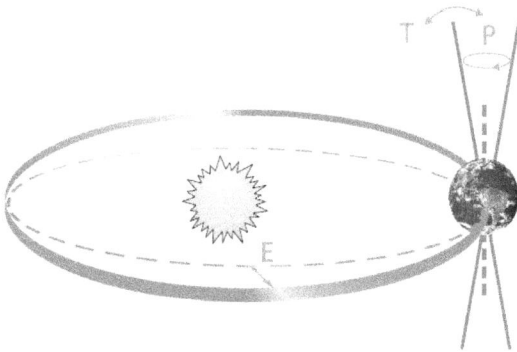

Milankovitch Cycles. *Schematic of the Earth's orbital changes (Milankovitch cycles) that drive the ice age cycles. 'T' denotes changes in the tilt (or obliquity) of the Earth's axis, 'E' denotes changes in the eccentricity of the orbit (due to variations in the minor axis of the ellipse), and 'P' denotes precession, that is, changes in the direction of the axis tilt at a given point of the orbit. Source: Rahmstorf and Schellnhuber (2006).*

Source: Rahmstorf and Schelinhuber, 2006

This 100,000 year long cycle was created by the earth's orbit characteristics - precession (axial rotation), obliquity (axial tilt), eccentricity (orbit shape), and solar forcing. Those four factors run on different cycle and fluctuation. Once combining the effects of those 4 factors, they create earth's temperature cycle that matches perfectly well with the glacial cycle. This amazing model was called Milankovic cycle.

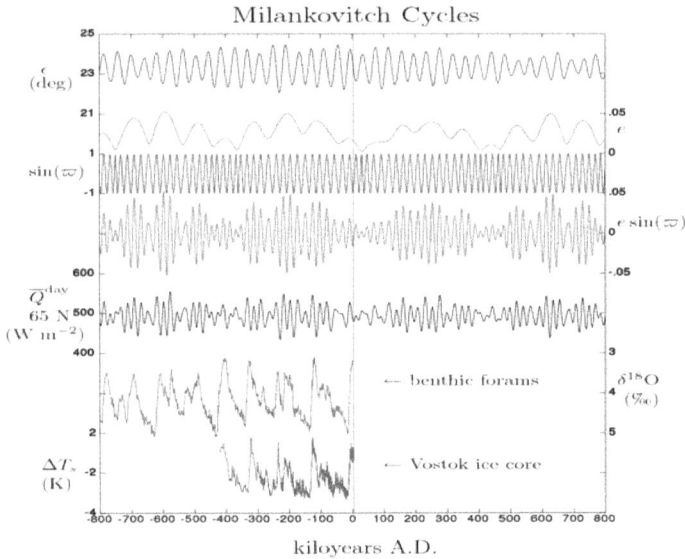

Milankovitch Cycles

Source: Milutin Milankovic

The most recent glacial age is consistent with the pattern of last 8 cycles. Earth entered this warm, inter-glacial age about 18,000 years ago. During previous 8 cycles, average inter-glacial time lasted about 15,000-20,000 years. Hence, we are near the end of this warm, inter-glacial cycle. Earth temperature is destined to be lower in the next 80,000 years.

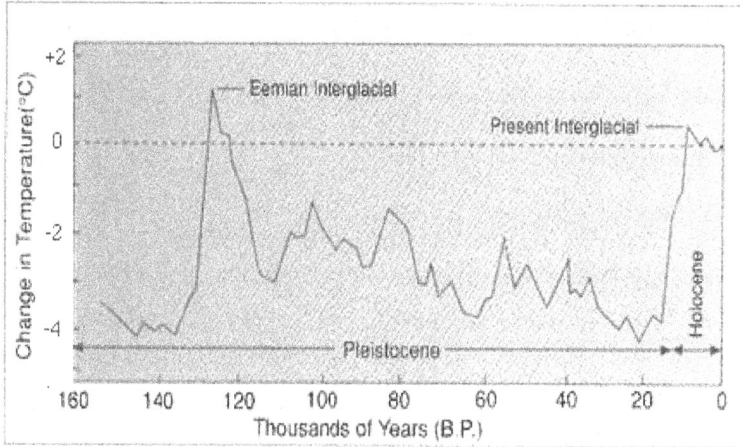

Source: Compiled by R.S. Bradley and J.A. Eddy based on J. Jouzel et al., Nature vol. 329. pp. 403-408, 1987 and published in Earth Quest, vol. 5, no. 1, 1991. Courtesy of Thomas Crowley.

Earth temperature has been rising in the last 18,000 years after the earth exited the most recent glacial age with the most rapid rise in the first 1000-2000 years. Sea level rose and life flourished since then. The claim that earth is heating up by burning fossils has to be analyzed within a context. Admittedly, CO_2 is a greenhouse gas, but its impact on earth temperature is the difference between the actual rise minus background rise, and minus impacts from other factors.

There are numerous self-correcting mechanisms in regulating earth temperature. Even burning fossil fuels can generate earth-cooling effects. Not long ago in 1970s, environmentalists, like Stephen Schneider, of the National Center for Atmospheric Research in Boulder, Colorado feared anthropogenic atmospheric pollution could block the sun and reduce earth temperature. Dusts from coal burning could form tiny aerosol particles that blocked the sun's radiance, which offset the greenhouse effects of CO_2.

Also, many natural events can reduce earth temperature; for example, the volcano eruption at Pinatubo Mount in June 1991 reduced the global temperature by about $0.5^{\circ}C$ in following 2 years.

Between 1940 and 1970, the global average temperature did in fact appear to be cooling. (see the chart by Polyakov, 2004.) Then surprisingly - in the late 1970s the temperature stopped declining and surface temperatures during the 1980s and 1990s began reading small but steady increases from ground-based stations. Climate fears of "global cooling" suddenly changed to "global warming".

What Determine the Surface Temperature of the Earth?
Average earth surface temperature is at $15^{\circ}C$, which is determined by the difference of incoming energy and outgoing energy. To understand the fluctuating earth surface temperature, we need to know what and how main factors affect the energy flow. How CO_2, as a greenhouse gas, play a role in affecting surface temperature becomes clear after we analyze those factors.

EARTH'S ENERGY BUDGET

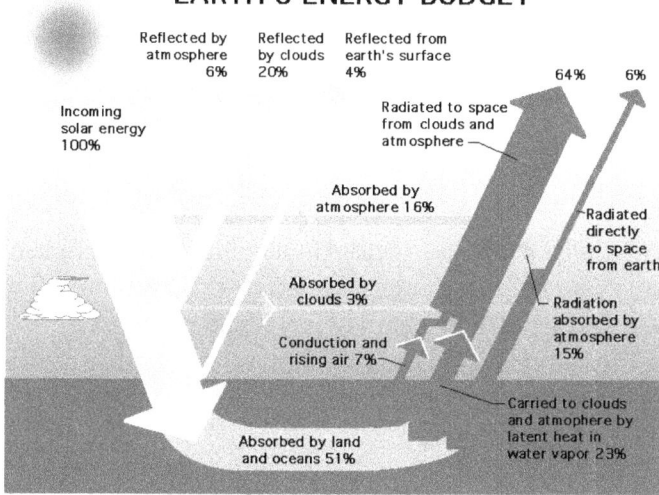

Source: NASA http://asd-
www.larc.nasa.gov/erbe/components2.gif

Earth surface received radiation from the sun, at the upper
atmosphere at an intensity of 1,367 watt/ per square meter. About
50% of that energy is absorbed by earth surface, 20% by
troposphere and stratosphere and rest 30% are reflected by clouds.
The surface then emits infrared radiation to release the energy,
which was subsequently absorbed by greenhouse gases in the
troposphere.

	Perihelion	Aphelion	Mean
Direct Solar	1414 W/sqM	1323 W/sqM	1367.5 W/sqM
Albedo	0.30+/-0.01	0.30+/-0.01	0.30+/-.01
Planetary IR	234 +/-7 W/sqM	234+/-7 W/sqM	234 +/7 W/sqM

Source: *Thermal Environments JPL D-8160.*
http://www.tak2000.com/data/planets/earth.htm

The energy absorbed by troposphere was radiated back to earth surface, which cause a surprise fact that earth surface radiate more energy than it received from the sun. Hence, troposphere is indeed a blanket covering the earth and most of that effect is from greenhouse gases. Without this blanket, earth temperature will be around $-18^{\circ}C$ and no life can survive.

Radiative forcing of greenhouse factors is the difference between incoming energy and outgoing energy, relative to the year 1750. CO_2's radiative forcing of 1.66 means that CO_2 kept outgoing radiation by 1.66 watt per square meter relative to the amount in 1750. Radiative forcing is used to quantify the effects from various factors in trapping energy.

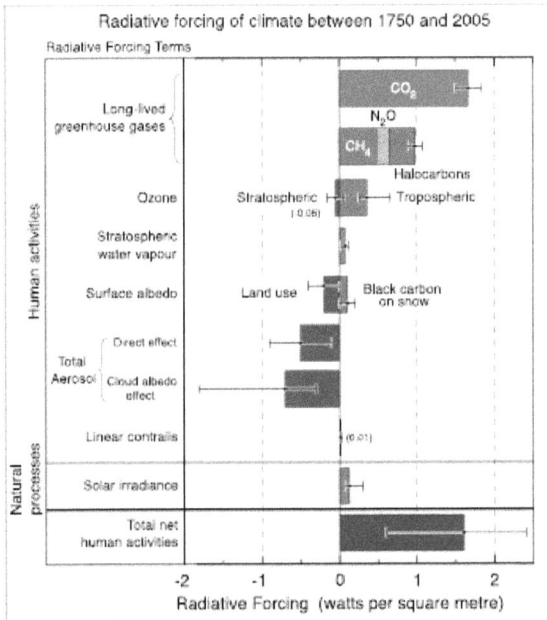

Source: IPCC 2007

Based on Forster etc. study, total radiative forcing relative to 1750 is 2.99 watt/m^2, with CO_2 at 1.66, and CH_4 at 0.48. For CH_4, its concentration has varied between 0.4 to 0.7 ppm by volume in last 800,000 year through glacial cycles. Its current concentration is 1.75 ppm, and remained constant in last 2 decades. Over a 100-year period, Methane (CH_4) is 21x times more potent in trapping heat in the atmosphere than CO_2, according to the IPCC report.

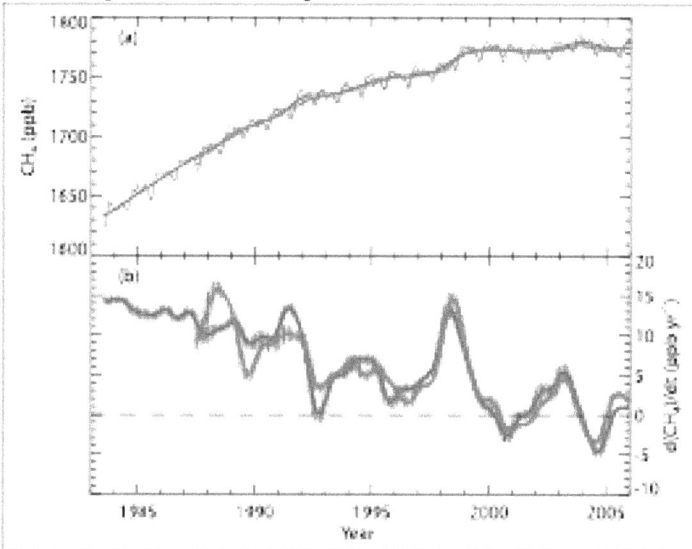

Source: Climate Change 2007: *The Physical Science Basis* and EPA

CO_2 accounts for more than half of greenhouse effects. Since 1958, atmosphere CO2 has been continuously measured at Mauna Loa Observatory in Hawaii. Due to the planting season in north hemisphere, CO_2 fluctuates by 5 ppm each year from Apr. to Oct. In 50 years, average CO_2 concentration has been rising steadily from 315 ppm in 1958 to 385 ppm in 2009.

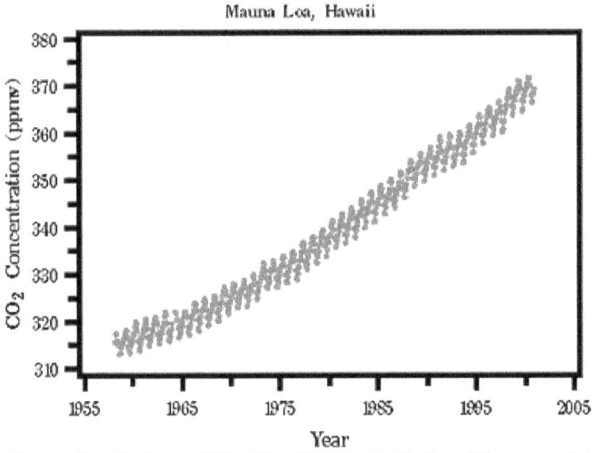

Mauna Loa, Hawaii

Source: Dave Keeling and Tim Whorf (Scripps Institution of Oceanography)

Source: Scripps Institution of Oceanography

Longer term CO_2 level in atmosphere can be measured by ice core samples. In Antarctic, snow falls on snow each year. Some of those have not melted in last million years. Air sample from each year was trapped among ice particles.

Ice core drilled from East Antarctic ice sheet, scientists were able to back measure atmospheric concentration of CO_2 back to past 800,000. The time interval covered 8 glacial-interglacial cycles. And resolution of the timeline was 1,000 years.

Do CO_2 Emissions Cause Global Warming

This is the most striking chart that has been used to illustrate the close relation between temperature and CO_2. The rise and fall of the temperature almost perfectly CORRELATED with CO_2 concentration. Al Gore and the rest of the global warmists use this ice core data to convince the world that if we raise the CO_2 concentration, earth temperature will follow.

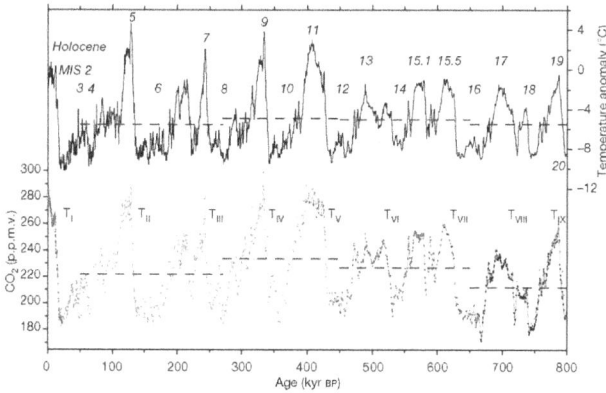

Source: Dieter Lüthi, etc. Nature 453, 379-382(15 May 2008)

This conclusion is seriously FLAWED!

This chart demonstrated only the close correlation between CO_2 from ice core and calculated earth temperature. Because the resolution is 1000 years, we do not know which factor is leading the move. Did CO_2 rise follow temperature rise, or vice versa?

Close inspection of the data and other studies have suggested that the CO_2 changes LAG temperature changes by centuries, although this lag was not clear in the Luthi's graph due to the resolution of the data.

Hence, warming might be initiated by other reasons, and CO_2 might be released from ocean water when temperature rose. During the 800,000 years, CO_2 fluctuated between 170-300 ppm. Current level as of 2008 was 382ppm, exceeding the highest level. Apparently, the rising of CO_2 during those cycles could not be attributed to human activities. Dinosaurs did not burn any coal or crude oil. Mostly likely, the rising CO_2 was the result of, not the cause of rising temperature. And earth temperature fluctuated in cycles according to Milankovic cycle.

Rising CO_2 could be the result of releasing dissolved CO_2 in the ocean because of higher temperature in the atmosphere and the ocean. As water temperature rises, CO_2 is released to the atmosphere, very much like opening a can of Coke. Ice core data did NOT prove that rising CO_2, from anthropogenic activities, would cause rising temperature on earth. They only showed the historical synchronized movement between CO_2 and temperature.

Carbon reservoirs and cycle on earth surface are well summarized in this chart.

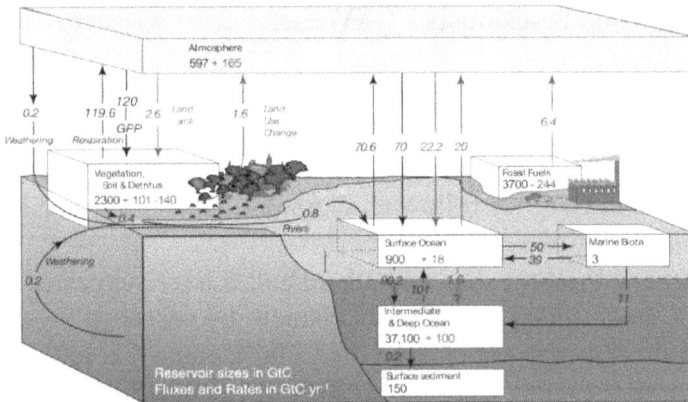

Source: *IPCC AR4 (2007) Fig 7.3.* and by Joseph Priestley and Antoine Lavoisier; and L.R. Kump etc. *The Earth System*, 2nd edition

There are almost equal amounts of CO_2 in the atmosphere and in the ocean surface water (760 billion tons and 1,050 billion tons respectively) and much more in the ocean as bicarbonate ions and sediment rocks. Carbon circulates among those forms in a short-term cycle, and a long term cycle. Long-term cycle refers to the movement between solid rock/fossil form and ocean/air form. Over millions of years, carbon entering reservoir through formation of rocks and fossils exceeded carbon released from reservoir. Hence, the CO_2 concentration in atmosphere today is much lower than it was 500 million years ago. Through this long cycle, the balance among reservoirs determined CO_2 concentration in the air.

Phanerozoic Carbon Dioxide

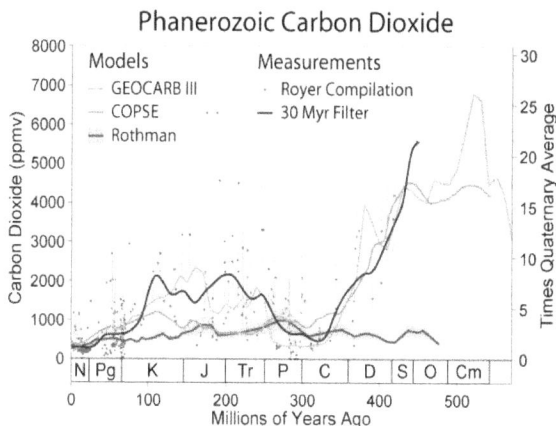

Source: GEOCARB, Berner and Kothavala, *American Journal of Science* 304: 397–437. 2001; COPSE, Bergmann et al. *American Journal of Science* 301: 182-204. 2004.

Short-term cycle refers to the movement of carbon among air, water, soil and biosphere, which usually takes months to years to reach equilibrium. In this short cycle, photosynthesis and physical dissolution moves carbon around. On average carbon molecules reside in atmosphere for about a decade.

Burning fossils fuel and cement production bring CO_2 out of its huge, long-term reservoir to its transient reservoir, which is the air and ocean water. In 2007, 29 billion tons of CO_2 were released into the air from burning fossil fuels. CO_2 from burning fossil fuels, despite its huge tonnage numbers, was only a small fraction of CO_2 emitted by plant decay. Admittedly, plant decay emissions are balanced by plant growth each year, and burning fossils is a one-way street that is additive to CO_2 in the air.

Can increased CO_2 emission be offset somehow? Carbon storage and sequestration technology are still under development. Fortunately, nature already has its own negative feedback mechanism to offset elevated CO_2.

First of all, plant growth will be better. Land plant growth in the nature is constrained by CO_2. CO_2 is food and nutrient for plants. Assuming other nutrients are given adequately, increased CO_2 will enhance plant growth. We know that plants in greenhouse grow faster and bigger, under a CO_2 concentration of ~1,000-1400 ppm. Increased biomass growth will meaningfully reduce CO_2 level in the atmosphere.

Second, ocean will absorb more CO_2 if its level in the air is elevated. The balance of CO_2 between air and water is governed by physical law - temperature and relative concentration. As more CO_2 accumulates in the air, more CO2 will be dissolved in the water. Increased CO_2 in dissolved form will also help plankton and shell animal growth, which eventually deposit as carbonate on the ocean floor.

This mechanism of CO_2 absorption was researched and published in Science 305 (2004) by Chris Sabine etc. Of all human made CO_2 emission since industrial age, 48% of them have been absorbed by the ocean. Of course, this is NOT an excuse for us to continue burning fossil fuels.

Nevertheless, the impact of CO_2 on global temperature is vastly exaggerated. All we know so far is that

- ✓ CO_2 concentration rose from 280 ppm to 380 ppm in last 100 years
- ✓ Global temperature increased by $0.5^0C \sim 0.7^0C$ at the same period (according to Hansen)
- ✓ Highly synchronized movement of temperature and CO_2 in last one million years.

But, we do not know which one is the cause, which one is the effect. Earth temperature rises and falls, depending on many factors. Many of these factors are beyond our control, such as solar spot activities and glacial cycles. The cycle of solar spot activity, which is beyond the scope of this article, is another important factor affecting the earth temperature. Additionally, sampling bias and statistical errors can totally distort results, despite available facts and data.

Misplaced emphasis on CO_2 as the culprit of rising earth temperature

By now, it is clear that earth temperature is determined by a myriad of factors with solar radiation being the most important one. Greenhouse gases are secondary factors that keep earth warm, but they are also subject to influence from human activities. Of the greenhouse gases, this is the order of importance:

1. Water vapor
2. CO_2
3. Methane
4. NOx, SOx, and other

Why are we so obsessed with CO_2? And point fingers to an obviously misplaced target? Should we focus on cloud formation? And methane?

A fortunate thing about the atmosphere is that there is a negative feedback system between clouds and temperature. If the earth temperature rises, more water vapor will accumulate in the air. More cloud will form if water vapor is increased. Clouds reflect solar radiation back to space and hence, reduce energy reaching earth surface. We are lucky to have white clouds and blue sky.

Additionally, one shocking fact about methane was pointed out by Steve Levitt in his best selling book *Superfreakonomics*. He said it was generally believed that CO_2 generated from cars and airplanes heated up the earth. However, when we raise cow for beef, the cow's dung will generate methane. Methane is 25x more potent as a greenhouse gas than CO_2. The world ruminants are responsible for about 50% more greenhouse effects than the entire transportation sector!

Irreversible Process? Try Geo-Engineering!

Al Gore: "We face the gravest threat that civilization has ever confronted. It's global in nature and requires a global solution. Increased CO_2 emissions anywhere, whether from China or the United States or from one of the countries that is burning its forests like Brazil or Indonesia—from wherever the emissions come, they have the same effect: They trap much more heat from the sun, melt the ice, raise the sea level, cause stronger storms, floods, drought, bigger fires, generate millions of climate refugees, destabilize political systems, threaten the growing of food crops and cause a number of other catastrophic consequences which, taken together, threaten the basis for the future of human civilization on the Earth. Because these consequences are distributed globally, the problem masquerades as a distraction. Because the length of time between causes and consequences stretches out longer than we're used to dealing with, it gives us the illusion that we have the luxury of time. Neither of those things is true. The crisis is a concrete threatening reality today. It stands to get catastrophically worse unless we take action before the accumulation [of] this global warming pollution reaches such toxic levels that the problem becomes bigger than we can solve.

We're already at the point where it's stretching our capacity to reach an agreement that will solve the problem, but it's still within our capacity. There are abundant reasons for hope that we will act in time. If you look at the difference between today and 10 years ago, there is a global consensus. More than 70 leaders from nations are gathering at Copenhagen. Many nations have taken action and the world is waiting for the natural leader, the United States to move on this."

In 2003 James Hansen published a paper called *Can We Defuse the Global Warming Time Bomb* where he argued, "human-caused forces on the climate are now greater than natural ones, and that this, over a long time period, can cause large climate changes." His view on actions to mitigate climate change is that "halting global warming requires urgent, unprecedented international cooperation, but the needed actions are feasible and have additional benefits for human health, agriculture and the environment."

In a 2009 book, Hansen said, "Planet Earth, creation, the world in which civilization developed, the world with climate patterns that we know and stable shorelines, is in imminent peril. The urgency of the situation crystallized only in the last few years. We now have clear evidence of the crisis, provided by increasingly detailed information...." And that "the startling conclusion is that continued exploitation of all fossil fuels on Earth threatens not only the other millions of species on the planet but also the survival of humanity itself - and the timetable is shorter than we thought. "

It seemed doom and gloom after listening to James Hansen and Al Gore. Even more depressing is that the COP15 in Copenhagen failed terribly and politicians from many countries were shortsighted as they cared only about re-election and GDP growth in their few years term. People are burning coal and oil more feverishly than they ever did. Are we heading to hell's day on Earth?

In June 1991, Pinatubo Mount in Philippine, erupted intense sulfuric ash into the sky for 9 hours. It was the second most powerful eruption in the 20th century. Within 2 hours, sulfuric ash reached 22 miles high, discharged 22 million tons of sulfuric oxide to the stratosphere.

In following 2 years, heavy sulfuric ash acted a blanket for the region, and reduced world temperature by 0.5^0C! Isn't that ironic? An unexpected Pinatubo volcano can reverse the entire rise of earth temperature caused by global industrialization. If the impact of sulfuric oxide was true, can we create an artificial volcano eruption to reverse the rise of global temperature?

Actually, a scientific solution can be much more elegant. **Geoengineering** is a large-scale engineering of our environment, including soil, ocean, and atmosphere, in order to combat or counteract the effects of changes in earth's climate system.

© Copenhagen Centre

Source: nextnature.net and infowars.net

In 1956, a report called *Restoring the Quality of Our Environment* was drafted by US President's Science Advisory Committee. It was the first high-level recommendation of a geo-engineering solution to modify earth's heat balance. "The possibility of deliberately bringing about countervailing climate changes…need to be thoroughly explored"

In 1991, a 917-paged book called *POLICY IMPLICATIONS OF GREENHOUSE WARMING* was published by a Committee on Science, Engineering, and Public Policy, National Academy of Sciences, National Academy of Engineering, Institute of Medicine. The book presented methods for assessing options to reduce emissions of greenhouse gases into the atmosphere, to assist humans and unmanaged systems of plants and animals adjusting to the consequences of global warming, and to mitigate the effects of greenhouse gas emission. "Undertake research and development projects to improve our understanding of both the potential of geoengineering options to offset global warming and their possible side effects. This is not a recommendation that geoengineering options be undertaken at this time, but rather that we learn more about their likely advantages and disadvantages."

In 2002, Dr. Edward Teller, a Nobel Laureate responsible for the hydrogen bomb, submitted a article to National Academy of Engineering, with colleagues Roderick Hyde and Lowell Wood, suggested that geoengineering solution, not CO2 reduction, "is the path mandated by the pertinent provisions of the UN Framework Convention on Climate Change"

Failure of COP15 for countries to sign up for a CO2 reduction supported the need to develop a geoengineering solution. Emerging economies, particularly China and India, are heavily relying on coal to power their economies. Brazil is fortunately powered by hydro and Russia by natural gas. USA is also reluctant to cut emissions because 50% of its electricity is generated by coal. Despite repeated, tenacious efforts from global environmentalists and Al Gore, COP15 did not reach any tangible goals. That should not surprise anyone because science is NOT settled.

Belarusian climate scientist named Mikhail Budyko first suggested spreading sulfur dioxide (SO_2) in the stratosphere, to create sulfate particles that could replicate the effect of volcano eruption at Pinatubo Mount. Budyko's 1956 book, *Heat Balance of the Earth's Surface*, transformed climate research from a qualitative into a quantitative physical science. His new physical methods, based on earth heat balance, were quickly adopted by scientists in the world. By scientists' estimate, 100,000-600,000 tons of SO_2 per year will be sufficient to counter the warming trend.

Additionally, Yuri Israel, the former Vice Chairman of IPCC, and Head of Institute of Global Climate and Ecology Studies at

Moscow, sent a letter to President Vladimir Putin and suggested conducting a small-scale experiment of shooting SO_2 to the air.

How to spread sulfur dioxide is a technical issue. There are many ways to conduct the experiment. The critical message is that geo-engineering can save the earth. We are not doomed by burning coal. Even if we burn all proven reserves of fossil fuels in one single day, the earth will be NOT destroyed – ocean will absorb half of the CO2, and plant growth will be better, although atmospheric CO2 may rise. Plant will yield 70% more mass if CO2 level is raised to 1200ppm (typical at commercial greenhouse) from 380ppm, assuming other conditions are equal. Temperature may be slightly higher, but it is reversible by spreading SO_2.

IPCC estimated that in 2100, earth temperature might be 2^0C ~ 6^0C higher than today, depending on which model they use. While readers may be scared by the forecast rise of temperature by IPCC, scientists already have solutions. In a report by *The Swedish Society for Nature Conservation*, they listed ten new ways to geoengineer the planet:

1. Create vast monoculture tree plantations for biochar, biofuels & CO_2 sequestration;
2. Contaminate Centres of Genetic Diversity with DNA from genetically engineered crops;
3. Fertilize the ocean with iron nanoparticles to increase phytoplankton that theoretically sequester CO2;
4. Proliferate nuclear power plants
5. Build 16 trillion space sunshades to deflect sunlight 1.5 million km from Earth
6. Launch 5,000-30,000 ships with turbines to propel salt spray to whiten clouds to deflect sunlight

7. Drop limestone into the ocean to change its acidity so that it can soak up extra CO2
8. Store compressed CO2 in abandoned mines and active oil wells;
9. Biannually, blast sulfate-based aerosols into the stratosphere to deflect sunlight;
10. Cover deserts with white plastic to reflect sunlight

Stern Review And His $1.2 Trillion Solution: On October 30th 2006, economist Nicholas Stern sent a 700-page report to UK government, detailed climate change and its economic impact. It is the most comprehensive study and was widely discussed, both positively and negatively. Here are few excerpts of his conclusion:

"There is still time to avoid the worst impacts of climate change, if we take strong action now. The scientific evidence is now overwhelming: climate change is a serious global threat, and it demands an urgent global response. Climate change will affect the basic elements of life for people around the world – access to water, food production, health, and the environment. Hundreds of millions of people could suffer hunger, water shortages and coastal flooding as the world warms."

"Using the results from formal economic models, the Review estimates that if we don't act, the overall costs and risks of climate change will be equivalent to losing at least 5% of global GDP each year, now and forever. If a wider range of risks and impacts is taken into account, the estimates of damage could rise to 20% of GDP or more. In contrast, the costs of action – reducing greenhouse gas emissions to avoid the worst impacts of climate change – can be limited to around 1% of global GDP each year."

He suggested the world to spend 1% GDP to develop new technologies, change economic structure, and reduce CO_2 emission. In 2008, he raised his price tag to 2% of global GDP, or $1.2 trillion to fulfill the CO_2 and temperature goal.

$1.2 trillion?! Maybe $1.2 trillion will do the work. Like many other problems, there are always solutions, but the issue is cost. If we stop all economic activities and return to Stone Age, we can surely stop emitting CO_2. Is that what we want?

What about a $250 million geo-engineering solution?

It is not time to implement geo-engineering solutions yet, but we should prepare a Plan B to save the earth in case all scares of global warming turn out to be true. Given that impacts from geo-engineering may not be reversible and have a global consequence, we should be careful in designing and testing the solution, because we cannot conduct a large scale experiment without impacting the earth.

If the warming continues, which is unlikely and doubtful, sea level may rise to a disaster level so that hundreds millions people have to migrate inland from world's coastal cities. Those solutions will be needed when New York, London, Hong Kong are under water and people have to swim for grocery shopping. Still, there is no urgency to implement the solution. For now, let's test and develop those solutions, and keep the know-how in a closet.

Finally, in another millennium or so, earth will enter the next glacial phase that will definitely cool down the earth, and this global warming fever.

About Author

Jeff Lumin is a venture investor, entrepreneur and business writer. He was trained as a scientist in physiology, and started his career as a research analyst and fund manager with leading institutional investors - AIG, Franklin Templeton, and CITIC Securities. He spent decades investing in global biotech, pharmaceutical and device companies, and built investment record in companies at early stage of drug development, and in evaluating those life science assets.

During financial crisis, Jeff worked at the investment division of CITIC Securities, China's leading investment bank. He conducted extensive cross-country research, comparing major countries on: macro-economic policy, fiscal/taxation and tariff, industrial policy, labor force and education, political groups and election cycles. Jeff traveled to Russia, Brazil, Chile, Britain, France, Germany, Canada, US, Belgium, Switzerland to meet with political leaders and corporates' senior management, to conduct investment due diligences, and to visit companies' field operations and to experience local cultures. Those vertical and horizontal comparisons not only help Jeff to make investment decisions, but also to identify strength and weakness of those economies.

His previous publications include: "What Wall Street Missed" and "Transform China to a Consumption Economy". Jeff received MBA from Yale School of Management, and M.S. and M. Phil. degrees from Yale School of Medicine.

Printed in the United States of America

First Printing, Oct. 2017

ISBN 978-0-692-95455-3

www.ingramcontent.com/pod-product-compliance
Lightning Source LLC
Chambersburg PA
CBHW060033030426
42334CB00019B/2311